944.0280922
K68

MADISON AREA TECHNICAL COLLEGE IRC

00010150372 0

MA\

D0084535

FRENCH RE\

F

HIGHSMITH #45231

MATC-TRUAX-LIBRARY
3550 ANDERSON STREET
MADISON, WI 53704

MATC-TRUAX-LIBRARY
3550 ANDERSON STREET
MADISON, WI 53704

French Renaissance Monarchy: Francis I and Henry II

SECOND EDITION

R.J. KNECHT

LONGMAN
LONDON AND NEW YORK

Addison Wesley Longman Limited
Edinburgh Gate
Harlow
Essex CM20 2JE
England
and Associated Companies throughout the world.

*Published in the United States of America
by Longman Publishing, New York.*

© Longman Group Limited 1984, 1996

All rights reserved; no part of this publication may be
reproduced, stored in a retrieval system, or transmitted
in any form or by any means, electronic, mechanical,
photocopying, recording, or otherwise without either the
prior written permission of the Publishers or a licence
permitting restricted copying in the United Kingdom issued
by the Copyright Licensing Agency Ltd.,
90 Tottenham Court Road, London W1P 9HE.

First published 1984
Second Edition 1996

ISBN 0 582 287073 PPR

British Library Cataloguing-in-Publication Data
A catalogue record of this book is
available from the British Library

Library of Congress Cataloging-in-Publication Data
Knecht, R. J. (Robert Jean)
   French Renaissance monarchy: Francis I and Henry II/R. J.
Knecht – 2nd ed.
     p. cm. – (Seminar studies in history)
   Includes bibliographical references and index.
   ISBN 0 582 28707 3
   1. Francis I. King of France, 1494–1547. 2. Henry II, King of
France, 1519–1559. 3. Monarchy–France–History–16th century.
4. France–Kings and rulers–Influence. 5. Valois. House of–
Genealogy. I. Title. II. Series.
DC113.K584 1996
944'.028'0922–dc20
                                                        95–34669
                                                             CIP

Set by 7 in 10/12 Sabon
Produced through Longman Malaysia, TCP

CONTENTS

Editorial foreword   vii
Note on referencing system   viii
Acknowledgements   viii
Preface to the second edition   ix
Map   x

PART ONE: THE BACKGROUND

1. THE KINGDOM OF FRANCE   1

2. THE GOVERNMENT OF THE KINGDOM   12

PART TWO: ANALYSIS

3. THE MONARCHS: FRANCIS I AND HENRY II   24

4. FOREIGN AFFAIRS   30
    The Italian Wars   30
    Valois–Habsburg rivalry   33

5. THE SINEWS OF WAR   47

6. THE CHALLENGE OF HERESY   59
    The problem of definition   59
    The growth of persecution   67

7. THE KINGS AS PATRONS   73
    The royal court   73
    Francis I and Henry II as builders   76
    Francis I and Henry II as art patrons   80
    Literary patronage   83

PART THREE: ASSESSMENT

8. FRENCH RENAISSANCE MONARCHY:
    'POPULAR' OR 'ABSOLUTE'?   86

PART FOUR: DOCUMENTS 97

Genealogy: The House of Valois 120
Glossary 122
Bibliography 128
Index 134

EDITORIAL FOREWORD

Such is the pace of historical enquiry in the modern world that there is an ever-widening gap between the specialist article or monograph, incorporating the results of current research, and general surveys, which inevitably become out of date. *Seminar Studies in History* are designed to bridge this gap. The books are written by experts in their field who are not only familiar with the latest research but have often contributed to it. They are frequently revised, in order to take account of new information and interpretations. They provide a selection of documents to illustrate major themes and provoke discussion, and also a guide to further reading. Their aim is to clarify complex issues without over-simplifying them, and to stimulate readers into deepening their knowledge and understanding of major themes and topics.

ROGER LOCKYER

NOTE ON REFERENCING SYSTEM

Readers should note that numbers in square brackets [5] refer them to the corresponding entry in the Bibliography at the end of the book (specific page references are given in italic). A number in square brackets preceded by *Doc.* [*Doc.* 5] refers readers to the corresponding item in the Documents section which follows the main text. Words asterisked at first occurrence are defined in the Glossary.

ACKNOWLEDGEMENTS

The publishers would like to thank the following for permission to reproduce copyright material: Academie des Sciences Morales et Politiques for extracts from *Ordonnances des Rois de France: Regne de Francois Ier* 1936 and 1941 Vol V pp. 81–3 and Vol VII pp. 248–51; Yale University Press for an extract from *The Monarchy of France* by Claude de Seyssel, translated by J. H. Hexter, edited by D. R. Kelley, 1981; Phaidon Press Ltd for an extract from p. 125 of *The Autobiography of Benvenuto Cellini* edited and abridged by Charles Hope published in 1983.

PREFACE TO SECOND EDITION

In revising this book, I have taken note of important research done over the past decade. The chapter on the Sinews of War has been completely rewritten and that on the Kings as Patrons is new. A document has been added to illustrate this new chapter. The bibliography has been brought up to date.

R.J.K.

Birmingham, 1995

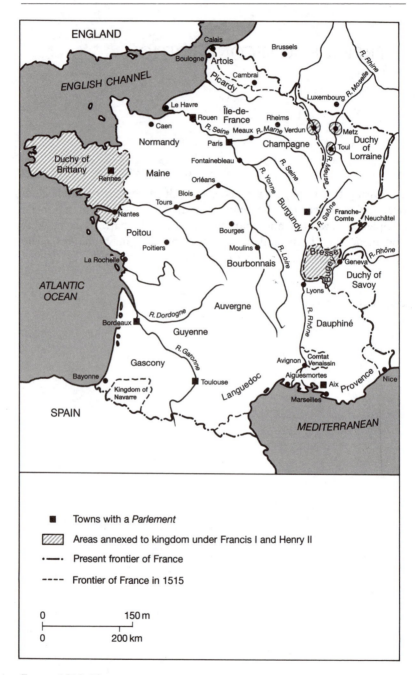

Towns with a *Parlement*

Areas annexed to kingdom under Francis I and Henry II

Present frontier of France

Frontier of France in 1515

0   150 m

0   200 km

France 1515–59

PART ONE: THE BACKGROUND

1 THE KINGDOM OF FRANCE

In 1515, when Francis I became king, France was still not a fully developed nation state. Signs of a national consciousness can be found in the writings of some contemporary scholars and also at a more popular level, yet France lacked well-defined frontiers, a common language and a unified legal system. Her eastern border was so blurred in places that some villagers living near it did not know whether they belonged to France or the Holy Roman Empire, a confusion which they happily exploited by evading taxes and the law. In so far as a frontier existed at all, it followed roughly the rivers Scheldt, Meuse, Saône and Rhône from the North Sea to the Mediterranean. People living west of this line were vassals of the French king; those to the east were subject to the emperor. French suzerainty over Artois and Flanders, however, was purely nominal, effective control of these areas having passed to the house of Burgundy. Further east, the frontier cut through the duchy of Bar, whose ruler, the duke of Lorraine, did homage for one half to the king of France, and for the other to the emperor. In the south, Dauphiné and Provence were still not regarded as integral parts of the kingdom, as they were situated east of the Rhône: the king was obeyed as dauphin in the one and as count in the other. The south-west border of France more or less followed the Pyrenees, avoiding Roussillon, which belonged to Aragon, and the small kingdom of Navarre, ruled by the house of Albret. Within France, there were three foreign enclaves: Calais, which belonged to England, the Comtat-Venaissin, which belonged to the papacy, and the principality of Orange, which belonged to the house of Chalon. A few great fiefs also survived, notably the duchy of Brittany and the large Bourbon demesne in central France.

Linguistically, too, France was not fully unified by the start of the sixteenth century. Modern French is descended from *langue d'oïl**, a dialect spoken in northern France during the Middle Ages; in the

*Asterisked words are explained in the Glossary on p. 122

south *langue d'oc** was used. After 1450, however, as the French monarchy asserted its authority, following the expulsion of the English from Gascony, the *langue d'oïl* began to make deep inroads in the south. The *Parlements** of Toulouse, Bordeaux and Aix used it, and southern noblemen who took up offices at court adopted it. They continued to speak it when they returned home and communicated the habit to their servants. By 1515 the expansion of the French language southward was in full swing: only Gascony, Provence and a few smaller areas needed to be won over.

Another area where unification was less than complete at the end of the Middle Ages was the law. During the medieval period each province, often each locality, had its own set of customs. Broadly speaking, Roman law prevailed in the south, while customary law held sway in the north, but patches of customary law existed in the south and Roman law penetrated the north to a limited extent. For a long time customs were fixed by practice only: this made for flexibility, but also uncertainty. From the twelfth century, therefore, charters were drawn up listing the customs of individual lordships or towns. The first serious attempt at a more general codification was made by Charles VII (1403–61), but there was no general progress till Charles VIII set up a commission in 1497. It was under Louis XII (1462–1515) that codification really got under way and the process continued under Francis I.

During the first half of the sixteenth century France underwent a number of territorial changes. In the north-east, the town of Metz and the bishoprics of Toul and Verdun were occupied by France in 1552 and thereafter remained under the 'protection' of her king [123]. The duchy of Savoy was occupied militarily by the French from 1535 until 1559. Calais was permanently wrested from the English in 1558. But these gains have to be offset against certain losses. Thus under the peace of Madrid (1525), as subsequently confirmed by the treaties of Cambrai (1529) and Crépy (1544), France lost her rights over Flanders, Artois and Tournaisis – territories situated between the Scheldt and the North Sea.

Within the kingdom, the process of unification was advanced in the first half of the sixteenth century by the annexation of the duchy of Brittany and the absorption of the Bourbon demesne. It is often assumed that Brittany became part of France in 1491 as a result of the marriage between King Charles VIII and the duchess Anne. Actually, it was not until 1532 that the duchy was formally attached to the French kingdom. In 1515 Francis I had persuaded his first wife, Claude, who had inherited the duchy from Anne, her mother, to give him its administration. Thus ever since 1515 Brittany had been ruled by the king in the right of his wife. Then, in 1524, shortly before her death, Claude made a will bequeathing the duchy to her eldest son, François, but, as he was a minor, the king had continued to administer it. When François came of age in 1532, it became necessary to regularise its status. This was done with the consent of the local estates, which insisted on certain guarantees in respect of the duchy's rights and privileges. Under an edict of 1532 Brittany was irrevocably attached to France. By completing the process initiated forty-five years earlier, Francis made a notable contribution to French unification: from Calais to the Pyrenees the Atlantic seaboard now belonged to France.

Among the princely families that continued to hold sway over certain parts of France in the early sixteenth century the house of Bourbon was pre-eminent. It had been founded in the fourteenth century by a son of St Louis. In 1443 its lands in central France had been divided between the two sons of Duke Jean I, and for a time it looked as if the two branches of the family would go their separate ways. In 1488, however, the lands of the elder branch passed into the hands of Pierre de Beaujeu, who, having no son, bequeathed his property to his daughter, Suzanne. Her right to inherit, however, was challenged by her cousin Charles, head of the cadet branch of Bourbon-Montpensier. The dispute was submitted to the *Parlement* and an ingenious solution found: Suzanne and Charles were married, the lands of the two branches being thus reunited. In 1521 the Bourbon demesne comprised three duchies, seven counties, two *vicomtés** and seven lordships, forming an unusually compact block of territories in central France. Within his demesne, the duke was all-powerful: he could raise troops, levy taxes, dispense justice and summon the estates [52, I].

Charles of Bourbon was appointed constable of France* in 1515. As such, he became the effective leader of the French army in peacetime, but in 1521 a crisis in his relations with the king was precipitated by the death of the duchess Suzanne. She had made a will in her husband's favour, but its validity was challenged by the king's mother, Louise of Savoy, who claimed the inheritance as Suzanne's nearest blood relative, and by Francis, who argued that it had escheated to the Crown. Both claims were submitted to the *Parlement* and were vigorously contested by Charles and his mother-in-law, Anne de France. But the king did not wait for the *Parlement's* verdict before disposing of some of the duke's lands. This was certainly one reason for Bourbon's decision to turn traitor.

In 1523 he plotted with France's enemies, the emperor and the king of England, to lead a rebellion once Francis had invaded Italy. The plot, however, was discovered and the duke had to flee the kingdom. He was tried *in absentia* by his peers and all his property assigned to the Crown. In 1525 it was restored to him under the peace of Madrid, but he was unable to give effect to this, and in 1527 he was killed at the sack of Rome. This time, the Bourbon lands were divided between the king of France and his mother, and when she died in 1531, he acquired them all. In 1538 some of Bourbon's lands were restored to one of his sisters, but the bulk remained in the king's hands.

The surface area of France in 1515 was far smaller than it is today: 459,000 square kilometres as against 550,986. Yet it must have seemed enormous to people living at the time, for their communications were so primitive and slow by comparison with our own. Some idea of the speed of travel by road in the sixteenth century can be gained from a famous guidebook, *Le Guide des chemins de France* (1553). This shows that it was possible to cover 15 to 16 leagues (1 league equalled 3 miles or 4.8 kilometres) in a day where the terrain was flat, 14 where it rose gently, and 11 to 13 where it rose steeply. Thus it would have taken 2 days to travel from Paris to Amiens, 6 from Paris to Limoges, 7½ from Paris to Bordeaux, 6 to 8 from Paris to Lyons and 10 to 14 from Paris to Marseilles. In bad weather, of course, the speed of travel would be much reduced. Gilles de Gouberville, a small nobleman from Normandy who kept a diary, took 7 days to reach Blois – a distance of about 300 kilometres – in 1556. His average speed of travel was about 6 or 7 kilometres an hour.

To the sixteenth-century traveller France must have seemed not only a vast but also a largely empty country, for centres of population were mostly small and widely scattered. By modern standards the kingdom was thinly populated. No precise figures can be given because of the paucity of documentary evidence: no general census exists for this period and few parish registers survive [64]. Those that do are mainly concerned with Provence and the north-west, and are often in poor condition. They do not provide complete lists of baptisms, seldom record burials and mention marriages only sporadically. In so far as any overall estimate is possible, the population of France about 1515 was around 15 million (today it is 53,589,000). But, if small by present-day standards, it was growing. According to a contemporary, Claude de Seyssel, the increase in population could be seen in the towns and the fields. His account is supported by statistical evidence: a village with only 100 inhabitants in 1467 had 300 in 1503; another with only 1 in 1467 had 260 half a century later. Having been cut by a half between 1330 and 1450, the population of France apparently doubled between 1450 and 1560. The rise was not uniform throughout the kingdom: certain villages, even regions, maintained a high annual growth rate over a long period, while others made more modest gains. Even within a province there could be sharp local differences. Nor was the rise in population necessarily continuous. But the overall trend was upwards, so that by 1560 the population had returned to the same level as before the Black Death.

The main reason for the demographic upsurge after 1450 was a lessening of the misfortunes that had hit the French peasantry between 1340 and 1450. Outbreaks of plague still occurred from time to time, but there were no more pandemics of the kind that had swept France between 1348 and 1440. Epidemics were limited to one or two provinces at most and were less frequent. Three factors may explain the decline in the virulence of plague: partial immunity acquired through natural selection, an improved diet and preventive measures taken by many towns in the 1520s. Another scourge from which the countryside was largely freed after 1450 was war: except for certain border provinces, little fighting took place within France between the end of the Hundred Years' War and the start of the Wars of Religion. The absence of any major grain famine between 1440 and 1520 was another significant contribution to population growth.

The need to feed a growing population stimulated the recovery of French agriculture from the ravages of the Hundred Years' War. In many areas, notably the north-west and south-west, many villages had been wiped out and much cultivated land had gone to waste. The reconstruction of the land began in earnest about 1470 and continued till about 1540. It was left to the initiative of landlords, who had to overcome enormous difficulties: on many estates only 'thorns, thickets and other encumbrances' were visible; old boundaries had vanished and people no longer knew where their patrimonies lay. The task of compiling new terriers and *censiers** was costly and time-consuming. At first there was also a shortage of labour so that lords were obliged to offer substantial inducements to settlers on their land: serfs were emancipated and freemen, too, were granted concessions. The lot of the average peasant improved in consequence, while the seigneurial class found itself more hard-pressed than before.

The agricultural recovery, however, was the result of land-clearance and reclamation rather than improved techniques of farming. Consequently, the spectacular, albeit uneven, rise in grain production that followed the reconquest of the land soon ran out of steam. In the Île-de-France, for example, production slowed down after 1500, while in the Midi grain production reached a peak in the 1540s, then declined. In other words, agricultural growth ceased after the land had been reclaimed, and grain production, on which the French peasantry depended principally for its food, failed to keep pace with the rise in population. This helped to push up grain prices and to create grain shortages, which could be serious enough to cause starvation and death [*Doc. 9*]. In the Nantes region, for instance, there were grain famines in 1528–32, 1538 and 1543–45, the longest of them entailing a high death rate [48].

An unfortunate side effect of the demographic rise was the proletarianisation of the lower ranks of the peasantry. As long as farm-workers had been scarce, they had been well paid, but as they grew more numerous their wages failed to keep pace with rising grain prices. It has been estimated that the purchasing power of rural workers in the Paris region fell by 50 per cent between 1450 and 1550. Where the value of real wages fell dramatically, small peasant proprietors were driven to borrow money in order to buy food. Eventually, in order to settle their debts, they might be forced to sell their holdings, and the next step might be for them to lapse into vagabondage, one of the growing social evils of the time [**66**]. The activities of large gangs of vagabonds, who overran the countryside plundering and spreading terror, are frequently mentioned in contemporary chronicles. Not all were dispossessed peasants; many were troops disbanded after a campaign. Royal concern at their activities was reflected in a long series of edicts. Some forbade soldiers to claim 'vagabonds' as their 'servants', while others ordered vagabonds to move about only in small groups on pain of being 'cut to pieces'. But these measures proved ineffective: vagabondage in the wake of armies remained a serious problem till the end of the century.

Urban reconstruction was also under way at the time of Francis I's accession. Thus Paris, which was by far the largest town in France, more than recovered its population of before the Black Death (200,000). It may even have doubled by the mid-sixteenth century. Lyons' population rose from about 20,000 in 1450 to 80,000 in the 1550s. Rouen, Bordeaux and Toulouse went up from 20,000 in the late fourteenth century to 60,000, 50,000 and 40,000 respectively by the mid-sixteenth century. Smaller towns showed a comparable increase [27; 40]. The rise in urban population was due not only to natural growth but also to immigration. Evidence for this may be found in apprenticeship or marriage contracts and in the registers of admissions to hospitals. Out of 15,101 patients admitted to the Hôtel-Dieu in Lyons between 1520 and 1563, under 40 per cent were natives of the city; the rest were outsiders, mainly from neighbouring provinces. They included many apprentices, journeymen and servants, who were attracted to the city because of its freedom from gild controls.

Three towns – Paris, Lyons and Rouen – ranked with some of the largest in western Europe. Below them were ten or so with about 20,000 inhabitants each. Then there were some thirty towns with 10,000 inhabitants each, and lastly a large number of small towns with a few thousand. The character of each town was determined by its main activity. Trade was important to all of them, but some were also administrative, intellectual and ecclesiastical centres. Eight towns had *parlements*, about 90 were capitals of *bailliages** or *sénéchaussées**, 15 had universities and about 110 were archiepiscopal or episcopal sees. Virtually the only industrial towns at the beginning of the sixteenth century were Amiens, where the manufacture of cloth kept half the population employed, and Tours, where silk was important. They were soon joined by Lyons.

Contemporaries tended to divide urban society into three groups: the well-to-do (*aisés**), the proletariat (*menu peuple**) and the poor. The reality, however, was more complex. Apart from the nobility and clergy, which were not specifically urban categories (they were exempt from urban taxes and service in the militia), the upper end of the social scale was made up of wealthy merchants and officeholders. In towns like Bordeaux and Toulouse, which had a *parlement* yet were important in international trade, the two groups were fairly evenly balanced, but in others, like Lyons, where trade was all-important, the merchants were pre-eminent: they owned comfortable town houses and estates in the neighbouring countryside which yielded revenues that they added to the profits of their trade. In towns which were primarily administrative centres, officeholders were the dominant social group; they were often as rich as the merchants from whose ranks many of them had risen. The core of urban society consisted of artisans and small to middling merchants. They worked for themselves, served in the urban militia, paid taxes, took part in communal assemblies and owned enough property to guarantee their security in the future. Although not immune to the indirect effects of food shortages, they could count on having their daily bread at least. The lowest stratum of urban society – the *menu peuple* – consisted of manual workers, who were debarred from any share of local government and lived in daily fear of hunger. Francis I's reign marked the beginning of a serious decline in the living standards of the urban proletariat. The first five years saw the end of a 'golden age' of cheap bread. As from 1520 nominal wages began to lag behind grain prices [*Doc. 9*]. By the end of the century the purchasing power of the working man was 40 per cent less than at the beginning. Consequently, many of the *menu peuple* joined the ranks of the poor [*Doc. 10*].

The early sixteenth century saw some interesting developments in poor relief. During the Middle Ages poor relief other than private almsgiving had been of two kinds: public handouts and hospitalisation. No distinction had been drawn between the impotent poor (i.e. those unable to help themselves) and sturdy beggars. All hospitals had been either ecclesiastical or private foundations; neither the state nor the municipal authorities had been responsible for them. But all this changed under Francis. As from 1518 the king set about reforming the hospitals and leper houses. The laicisation of hospitals was also encouraged. At the same time, municipal relief organisations, called *bureaux des pauvres** and *aumônes-générales**, were set up in certain towns. They were designed to bring relief to the poor in their own homes and funded out of taxes on the well-to-do. A good example of such an organisation was the *Aumône-générale* founded in Lyons after a grave famine in 1531. Two main aspects of its work were the care of orphans and the public distribution of bread [66].

The reign of Francis I has been called the 'springtime of French trade' [40 *p. 236*]. No statistics exist for the volume of French overseas trade in 1515, but it had certainly recovered from its stagnation during the Hundred Years' War. The annexation of Provence in 1481 was an event of major significance for French trade in the Mediterranean: though Marseilles was unable to wrest the monopoly of Levantine trade from Venice, it did establish links with ports in Italy, Spain, Rhodes and North Africa. The development of Marseilles can be traced in notarial records and port-books. Thus the yield from harbour dues rose from about 400 *livres** around 1500 to 1,300 in 1519–20, and to more than 3,000 in 1542. The annual average in the 1540s was 8,000 *livres*. The population of Marseilles shows a parallel rise: from 15,000 in 1520 to 30,000 in 1554. During the early sixteenth century new trade routes were opened up, notably to Egypt. The French Atlantic and Channel ports also recovered in the late fifteenth century and carried on an active trade with England, Spain, the Netherlands and Scandinavia. An important boost was given to trade in the Atlantic by the movement of European expansion overseas that the Portuguese and Spaniards had pioneered. Among the most important Atlantic ports were Rouen, Nantes, La Rochelle and Bordeaux. Rouen was the principal market for north-west France: in addition to distributing local produce, it served as a market for goods from all over France and overseas. Though it was not comparable to Antwerp as an international market, its sailors and merchants did travel widely in Europe and beyond, while many foreign merchants were among its inhabitants. Bordeaux's prosperity was due to the revival of the local vineyards, the rapid development of woad cultivation in the Toulouse region and an extraordinary upsurge of inland water traffic. In an average year it exported between 20,000 and 30,000 barrels of wine. Francis I's main contribution to the development of France's Atlantic coast was the foundation of Le Havre.

France was largely self-sufficient in the basic necessities of life – grain, wine, salt and textiles. In terms of value and tonnage, grain was her most important commodity. Foreign grain sometimes had to be imported in times of famine, but normally the kingdom produced enough for its needs and was even able to export it. Wine consumption increased enormously during the sixteenth century, as is shown by the rapid extension of vineyards in certain areas, the yield from duties on wine and the multiplication of taverns. Then, as now, wine was produced for export – particularly to England and the Netherlands – as well as the home market. The same was true of salt, which was produced in marshes along the Mediterranean and Atlantic coasts. England, the Netherlands and the Baltic states all imported French salt, mainly from Nantes and La Rochelle. The principal cloth-producing areas of France were Normandy, Picardy, Paris, Champagne, Berry, Poitou and Languedoc. Generally speaking, French cloth was of ordinary quality and cheap; it served the day-to-day needs of the lower orders of society. Even the best French cloth could not compete with certain foreign imports. For the finest linen France looked to the Netherlands and South Germany and for silks to Italy [40].

In the early sixteenth century people generally believed that a nation's wealth lay in its stock of bullion. This is why in March 1517 Chancellor Duprat, addressing an assembly of fifty-two representatives from the 'good towns' of the kingdom, outlined a programme of economic reform aimed at stopping the exportation of money from France [129]. He proposed a ban on imports of spices and drugs except through the kingdom's seaports, a ban on imports of woollen cloth, an obligation on French merchants to pay for two-thirds of their foreign purchases with French goods and on foreign merchants to accept such goods in exchange for two-thirds of their imports, a revaluation of the coinage, the unification of weights and measures, a ban on imports of luxury fabrics and furs, the regulation of inns and inn-keepers and a ban on gold and silver exports to the Holy See. This programme was too national in scope for the towns; their response was benightedly parochial [*Doc. 3*]. But the government stuck to its principles: many royal ordinances regulating imports and exports were issued and various attempts were made by the Crown to lessen dependence on foreign imports by encouraging home industries. Francis I's reign marked an important stage in the development of customs duties. These had orginally been levied on exports only, but Louis XI had introduced a 5 per cent duty on silk imports. In 1517 Francis extended this duty to imports of cloth of gold and silver and, later, to goldsmiths' work and jewellery. In 1543 he revived a duty on alum and later extended it to all spices and drugs. In 1544 the first French customs house (*douane**) was established. The introduction of the silk industry to Lyons was closely related to the policy of conserving the kingdom's bullion stock; if silk could be produced at home, there would be no need to use cash for its purchase abroad. In 1538 a merchant called Étienne Turquet was given a subsidy by the local authorities to enable him to set up looms for the manufacture of velvet. Other local merchants contributed funds to the venture and a company was formed, soon to be followed by others. By 1554 Lyons' silk industry was employing 12,000 workers. Four years later French merchants were importing less than a third or a quarter of the silks they had previously imported from Italy; they were buying Lyons silk instead at far less cost [61].

Mining also received official encouragement in France during the early sixteenth century, if only to remedy an acute shortage of silver. People were authorised to prospect in many parts of the country, but mainly in the centre. German miners were invited to settle in France on favourable terms. This movement in turn stimulated the metallurgical industries. Metalware, especially iron and steel, was not widely used, agricultural tools being still largely made of wood. Apart from a few basic iron pots, the greatest demand in peacetime was for nails and pins. In wartime, of course, arms were needed. As the best European arsenals (e.g. Milan after 1525) were controlled by the emperor, France had to make her own weapons. There was consequently a rapid development of French iron production under Francis I. In 1542 there were allegedly more than 460 forges in France of which more than 400 had been set up in the previous 50 years. Most of them made use of water power, except in Forez, where coal was already in use. For non-ferruginous metals France continued to depend on foreign imports.

Printing grew rapidly at the end of the fifteenth century. The first press was set up in Paris in 1470 and in Lyons in 1473. By 1500 more than 30 towns had presses, and in 1515 there were more than 100 printing houses in Lyons alone. The fact that Lyons was a city of 'free work' – that is, one in which no fee or masterpiece was required by artisan or entrepreneur – encouraged industrial enterprise. All that was needed to open a printing shop was capital. This, however, was enough to create a gulf between master-printers and their journeymen. Since a press and its type cost almost as much as one year's wages, most journeymen could not afford ever to become masters. As the masters tried to maintain or raise their profits by cutting down on labour costs, journeymen formed associations in defence of their standard of living. Occasionally they downed tools [49 *pp. 1–16*]. Following a strike of journeymen-printers in Lyons in April 1539, the local *sénéchal* banned all gatherings of more than five journeymen. This decision was endorsed by the king and, ten days later, the famous ordinance of Villers-Cotterêts abolished all confraternities* throughout the kingdom. Neither measure succeeded in restoring good industrial relations in Lyons. As for the confraternities, they too survived. In 1561 they were reminded that their funds should be used only for charitable or religious purposes [80].

The French economy in the first half of the sixteenth century was generally in good shape: agriculture had recovered from the crisis of the fourteenth century, urbanisation was growing apace, and trade, both domestic and international, was booming. Yet all was not well. The failure of agricultural production to keep pace with the needs of a fast-growing population was forcing many people on to the breadline. Similarly, inflation was reducing the real wages and living standards of the lower orders of society. Unemployment and vagabondage were serious problems and the state was being forced to intervene in order to solve or contain them [71]. From about 1520 France's prosperity was under attack; it did not, however, collapse until the second half of the century.

2 THE GOVERNMENT OF THE KINGDOM

Speaking to the Estates-General* of 1483, Philippe Pot, deputy of the nobility of Burgundy, recalled that the Crown was a dignity, not an inheritance. According to the jurists, it was handed down to the nearest male kinsman of the deceased king. The king was not free to give it away or to bequeath it to anyone of his choice; he was only the temporary holder of a public office. Yet the concept of the king as the head of the state already existed. Although the word 'state' did not come into current usage in France till the mid-sixteenth century, the idea of state did exist; but it was called the 'republic' or 'commonwealth' (*chose publique*). Official documents made a distinction between the king and the state, yet the interests of both were closely identified. Thus in 1517 the chancellor Duprat declared: 'the kingdom's interest is the king's interest, and the king's interest is the kingdom's interest. For it is a mystical body of which the king is the head.' In his capacity as head of the state, the king was not bound to assume the obligations entered into by his predecessor; the debts of one king could be repudiated by his successor. Any corporation or individual whose privileges had been recognised by the Crown needed to have them confirmed at the start of each reign. The same was true of royal office-holders.

'The king never dies.' This well-known adage conveys an important principle of French constitutional law: a monarch succeeded from the instant of his predecessor's death. There could be no interregnum, however brief. Nor could a lawful king be denied the full exercise of his authority for reasons either of age or health. If he was a minor or unable to rule for some other reason, his authority was to be exercised in his name by his council. In practice, however, a regent was appointed. In the sixteenth century this was usually a woman. Thus in 1515 and again in 1523 Francis I appointed his mother, Louise of Savoy, as regent, as he was about to leave on a military campaign in Italy, and in 1552 Henry II appointed his wife, Catherine de' Medici, as regent during his 'German voyage'.

By the sixteenth century the coronation or *sacre** at Rheims was no longer considered essential to the exercise of kingship [23; 75]. Yet it remained important as a symbol of the supernatural quality of kingship and of the close alliance existing between church and state. The coronation service began with the oath. Standing over the Gospels, the king promised to promote peace in Christendom, to protect Christians against injuries, to dispense justice fairly and mercifully, and to expel heretics from his dominions. This was followed by the anointing, the most important part of the ceremony. Thrusting his hand through specially contrived openings in the king's tunic and shirt, the archbishop of Rheims anointed his body with a chrism similar to that used for a bishop's consecration. This conferred on the king an almost sacerdotal character. Although no French king ever claimed the right to celebrate Mass, he did take Communion in both kinds, a privilege otherwise enjoyed only by priests.

By virtue of the anointing the king of France was deemed to have thaumaturgical* powers, that is to say, the power of healing sick people. The only other Christian ruler to claim this miraculous power was the king of England. Originally it was believed that the king could cure any disease, but by the sixteenth century his power had become restricted to scrofula (tuberculosis of the lymph nodes at the side of the neck), a disease more repulsive than dangerous and subject to periods of remission. The king touched the victims' sores and tumours with his bare hands, and, making the sign of the cross over each one, he said: 'The king touches you and God cures you.' Each was then given two small silver coins [29].

France in the early sixteenth century was still a largely feudal country: many towns, corporations and individuals enjoyed a measure of autonomy, regarding themselves as parties to a contract in which mutual obligations were laid down and total submission to the king was ruled out. But a school of thought existed which advocated royal absolutism. Its chief exponents were the royal jurists, who found in Roman law the idea of absolute power vested in one man and of subjects equally subservient to him. The doctrine of absolutism also received support from the Christian concept of the monarch as God's vicegerent on earth [42; 60]. The king, it was claimed, could legislate, dispense justice, revoke all lawsuits to his own court, levy taxes and create offices. It was his right to annul any concession detracting from his authority, and local privileges could survive only if he chose to renew them at his accession. Cicero's authority was invoked to show that the king was entitled to sacrifice private interest to the public good.

Two main currents of political thought existed in early sixteenth-century France: a moderate one, which advocated a close collaboration between the king and the sovereign courts (i.e. courts like the *Parlement* of Paris which had originally formed part of the *Curia Regis*), and an extreme one, which affirmed that only the king had the right to govern. These two currents are exemplified by two contemporary treatises: Claude de Seyssel's *La Monarchie de France* [16] and Guillaume Budé's *L'Institution du prince* [14]. Both were written for Francis I at the start of his reign. As an Aristotelian, Seyssel valued moderation in a constitution and admired the French monarchy precisely because he believed that it was tempered by the aristocracy, which he identified with the sovereign courts. The greatness of the kings of France, in his judgement, stemmed from their willingness to accept three restraints (*freins*) on their authority: religion, justice and *police*. By acting as a devout son of the Church, curbing judicial abuses and remembering his coronation oath, the king could prevent the monarchy from lapsing into tyranny [*Doc. 1*]. While sharing Seyssel's high regard for monarchy, Budé was prepared to allow the aristocracy only privileges, not a share of authority. Convinced as he was that royal authority was vested in the king alone, Budé attached great importance to his education. He advised the king to listen to wise counsellors, to respect his predecessors' ordinances, to safeguard the freedom and prosperity of his subjects and to abstain from war. Budé admitted, however, that the king was free to reject this advice, the only restriction on his power being the judgement of posterity [91].

But the power of the monarchy in Renaissance France, however absolute in theory, could not operate in a vacuum. An administrative machinery was needed, not only at the centre of the kingdom but in the provinces as well. Its chief component was the king's council, which at this time was still evolving. In theory its members comprised the princes of the blood, the peers of the realm and the great officers of state, but in practice admission to it was by royal invitation. In its widest form (*conseil d'état**), the council might have as many as twenty members. But there was also an inner ring (*conseil des affaires** or *conseil secret*), consisting of the king's close friends and advisers, whom he would consult on matters of special importance or requiring absolute secrecy, such as foreign affairs. The council's competence was universal and there was no specialisation among its members [53, I]. Since 1497, however, part of its judicial business had been transferred to the *Grand Conseil**, a tribunal with a fixed membership, which, like the council itself, continued to follow the king about the kingdom. The council also tended to leave financial technicalities to the king's fiscal officials.

The body responsible for turning the council's decisions into laws was the chancery, headed by the chancellor of France. Its staff comprised 119 king's notaries and secretaries whose office carried noble status. They drew up royal enactments and had them sealed by the chancellor, but, as government business increased in the sixteenth century, many conciliar decisions took the form of briefs (*brevets*) requiring only the signature of a notary or secretary to be valid [53, I]. What is more, as the central authority extended its sphere of activity, it became impossible for the king or the chancellor to keep tabs on everything. Consequently, a fair proportion of the decrees (*arrêts**) issued 'by the King and his council' were drawn up by the *maîtres des requêtes de l'hôtel**. Trained in the law, these officials played a role of growing importance in the state, linking up the various senior departments of the administration. They were recruited for the most part from among the office-holders, and a majority (there were about fifty in all for the reign of Francis I as a whole) improved their social standing by purchasing lordships (*seigneuries**) or being ennobled [53, I].

Some of the secretaries of state enjoyed the king's special confidence and were accordingly entrusted with drafting particularly important or confidential documents. Such was the expertise and knowledge of these *secrétaires des finances** that they were often called upon to give evidence to the king's council. Frequently, too, they were employed on diplomatic missions or given financial responsibilities. In April 1547 Henry II formally shared out government business among four *secrétaires des finances*, and soon afterwards they acquired the title of secretary of state (*secrétaire d'état*) to distinguish them from the rest of the royal notaries and secretaries [37].

In 1515 Francis I disposed of a handful of men – about 5,000 office-holders – to enforce his will throughout his kingdom; that is to say, one office-holder for every 115 square kilometres. If 3,000 subordinate officials are added to the total, the ratio becomes 1 royal administrator for every 60 square kilometres or 1 to 3,000 inhabitants (i.e. eleven times fewer than Louis XIV had to rule his twenty million subjects!). But in the course of his reign Francis I created many offices*, largely with a view to augmenting his revenues by selling them [94]. In 1546, a Venetian ambassador reported that 'offices are infinite in number and grow daily ... half of which would suffice'[94 *p. 41*].

The king was first and foremost a judge, and the earliest form of royal intervention at the local level had been the establishment of officials charged with exercising justice in his name. At the bottom of the hierarchy (but above the judges of the feudal courts) were magistrates, called *prévôts, viguiers* or *vicomtes*, whose powers were limited to the simplest cases. The basic unit of local government was the royal *bailliage* (sometimes called *sénéchaussée*). The kingdom comprised about 100 such units, which could vary enormously in size. By the sixteenth century the official in charge of the *bailliage*, namely the *bailli* (or *sénéchal*), had purely honorific or military duties. (e.g. he summoned the feudal levy, called the *ban-et-arrière-ban**), but the tribunal of the *bailliage*, under the *bailli*'s deputy or *lieutenant** and his staff, was a hive of activity, bustling with barristers, solicitors, sergeants and ushers. The *bailliage* judged on appeal cases sent up from inferior courts and in first-instance cases concerning privileged people (*privilégiés*) or 'cas royaux' (i.e. offences against the king's person, rights and demesne, ranging from treason and *lèse-majesté* to rape and highway robbery). In addition to their judicial competence, the *bailliages* had important administrative powers: they published royal statutes and issued decrees of their own. Under the edict of Crémieu (1536) their competence was more precisely defined and their authority over lesser courts reinforced [53, I].

Above the *bailliages* were the *parlements*, of which there were seven in 1515. The oldest and most prestigious was the *Parlement* of Paris, which had 'gone out of court' in the thirteenth century and was now permanently based in the old royal palace on the Île-de-la-Cité [89; 111]. Though separate from the king's council, it was still considered to be part of it: thus peers of the realm had the right to sit in it, and when the king came to the *Parlement*, accompanied by his ministers and advisers, to hold a *lit de justice**, the old *Curia Regis** was in effect reconstituted for the occasion. The *Parlement*'s view of royal absolutism differed from the king's: while admitting that authority resided in the king's person, it did not believe that he could treat the kingdom as he liked. He was its administrator, not its owner, and was bound to observe the so-called fundamental laws governing the succession to the throne and preservation of the royal demesne. The *Parlement*'s view implied a distinction between the sovereign as an ideal and the fallible creature who actually occupied the throne. It viewed its own role as that of protecting the interests of the ideal sovereign from the errors that the king, as a human being, might commit. The

Parlement's magistrates often compared themselves to the senators of ancient Rome, an analogy resented by the king.

In 1515 the *Parlement* of Paris consisted of five chambers (the *Grand' chambre**, two *chambres des enquêtes,* the *Chambre des requêtes* and the *Tournelle criminelle**) with a combined personnel of about sixty lay and clerical councillors. Under Francis I three chambers were added (two *chambres des enquêtes* and the *Chambre du domaine*) and the total number of councillors was doubled. There was a corresponding increase in the number of subordinate officials (ushers, sergeants, receivers and *procureurs**). In 1547, under Henry II, the notorious *Chambre ardente** was set up to deal with heresy cases, but it did not last beyond 1550 [*Doc. 19*]. In order to accommodate more offices than was warranted by the amount of judicial business facing the *Parlement,* Henry introduced in 1554 a system of biennial rotation, whereby twice as many councillors would serve for only six months in each year. This raised the total number to 165. But the system proved unworkable and had to be dropped in 1558. Yet another chamber (*Chambre du conseil*) was created to absorb the surplus councillors now that they all had to serve throughout the year!

Even allowing for the sharp rise in the number of *parlementaires**, the court was kept fully occupied, for its area of jurisdiction (*ressort*) covered two-thirds of the kingdom: it comprised the whole of northern France, excluding Normandy, as far south as the Lyonnais and Upper Auvergne. Within this area the *Parlement* judged a wide variety of cases in first instance and on appeal. But it was not just a court of law: it also regulated such matters as public hygiene or the upkeep of roads, bridges and quays; it ensured that Paris was adequately supplied with corn and fuel; it controlled the price, quality and weight of bread; it fixed wages and hours of work; it penalised shoddy workmanship; it censored books and it intervened in university affairs. Not even the Church escaped its vigilance: no papal bull could be applied in France without its being registered by the *Parlement.* It also kept an eye on the conduct of royal officials in the provinces. Finally, the *Parlement* played a significant role in politics by ratifying royal legislation. If an enactment was found by the *Parlement* to be satisfactory, it was registered and published forthwith; if not, it submitted objections or remonstrances* to the king, either verbally or in writing. He would either accept them and modify the proposed law accordingly, or he would refuse and issue a *lettre de jussion**, ordering the court to register the act as it stood without delay. Such a move might lead to more remonstrances and more *lettres de jussion*. In the end, if the Parlement declined to give way, the king would hold a *lit-de-justice*: that is to say, he would resume the authority he had delegated to the Parlement by coming to the court in person and presiding over the registration of the controversial measure himself [139]. Only the *Grand' chambre* was entitled to register royal enactments or to issue decrees (*arrêts*). Officially its head was the chancellor of France, but its effective head was the first president (*premier président**), who was assisted by three other presidents.

The provincial *parlements* developed out of the courts that had existed in the great fiefs before their absorption into the kingdom. Modelled on the Paris *Parlement*, they exercised a similar juris-diction within their respective areas. In 1515 there were six provincial *parlements*: Toulouse, Bordeaux, Dijon, Grenoble, Aix and Rouen. Brittany had *Grands Jours**, which did not become a fully fledged *parlement* till 1554. All these bodies claimed equality of authority and jurisdiction with that of Paris, but the latter had certain privileges making it unique. Each *parlement* was sovereign within its own area in respect of registering royal enactments: thus a law registered by the *Parlement* of Paris could not be applied in Languedoc unless it had also been registered by the *Parlement* of Toulouse. As in Paris, the personnel of the provincial *parlements* multiplied under Francis I: at Bordeaux, for example, the number of councillors and presidents rose from 29 to 66, and at Toulouse from 24 to around 80. But this increase in numbers matched the increase in the amount of legal business which the *parlements* had to cope with. It has been estimated that there were slightly more than 3,000 judges as compared with the total population of 15 million.

In January 1552 Henry II introduced a new tier of jurisdiction between the *bailliages* (or *sénéchaussées*) and the *parlements*. This consisted of sixty-one courts, called *présidiaux**, each with a staff of nine [53, I]. They were distributed unevenly in the jurisdictional areas of five *parlements* (Paris, Rouen, Rennes, Bordeaux and Toulouse). The purpose of the reform was ostensibly to save litigants time and money by freeing them from the need to under-take long and costly journeys to the *parlements*. But the real purpose was to bring more cash into the royal treasury by putting up another 500 offices for sale. The competence of the new courts in criminal matters was roughly similar to that of the *bailliages*, but in civil suits they could judge only cases involving property worth less than 250 or 500 *livres*. In June 1557 this limit was raised to 1,000 or 1,200 *livres*. At the same time each *présidial* was given a president, and soon a special chancery. As can be imagined, the *parlements* did not welcome a change which took away some of their business (and profits). Three times the *Parlement* of Paris refused to register the edict of 1552; in the end, it gave way only in return for face-saving concessions: the judgements of the new courts were to be called *sentences*, not *arrêts* (as in the *parlements*), and their seal was to display only one fleur-de-lys instead of three. Efforts made to extend the competence of the *présidiaux* ran into strong opposition, and the new courts never succeeded in establishing themselves firmly within the judicial hierarchy.

An exalted figure in French local government of the early sixteenth century was the provincial governor [68]. There were eleven governorships (*gouvernements**) corresponding roughly to the kingdom's border provinces. The governors were normally recruited from princes of the blood and high nobility: under Francis I they included the king's sons, brothers-in-law, uncle, favourites, the husbands of his mistresses and marshals of France. Although closely identified with the monarch's own person and authority, the governor was never more than a commissioner revokable at the king's pleasure. His powers, as stated in his commission or letters of provision, were seldom clearly defined. While it was customary for his military responsibilities (e.g. the securing of fortresses and the supplying or disciplining of troops) to be stressed, there was also frequently a clause open to wide interpretation. Thus in 1515 Odet de Foix, governor of Guyenne, was instructed 'generally to do ... all that we would see and recognize as necessary for the good of ourselves and our affairs ...' [13, I *p. 12*]. This was tantamount to a general delegation of royal authority. But there was no uniformity in the commissions of governors: it seems that the king was concerned rather with particular circumstances than with establishing functional harmony among his senior provincial representatives. As a governor was often at court or fighting for the king, he seldom resided in his province. The performance of his local duties was consequently delegated to a *lieutenant* – usually a lesser nobleman or prelate. But a governor could still do much for his province, even at a distance: he could, for example, ensure that its affairs received the attention of the king's council.

A governor's presence at court gave him unique opportunities of patronage which might be used to build up a powerful clientèle within his province. This comprised three elements: the regular army (*compagnies d'ordonnance**), household officers and servants, and local gentlemen. A governor did not have to be a captain of the *gendarmerie** (a collective name for the heavily armoured and mounted men-at-arms of the *compagnies d'ordonnance*), but nearly all the governors were captains. Though officially in the king's service and paid out of his treasury, the companies were tied to their captains, who controlled their recruitment and promotion within their ranks. A governor would also have a large private household capable of providing employment for local noblemen and an education for their children. All of this clearly made a governor potentially dangerous to the Crown. He might easily use his personal following within his province to undermine royal authority. In May 1542 Francis I annulled the powers of all governors on the ground that they had become excessive, but his move, it seems, was nothing more than a courteous way of depriving Anne de Montmorency, who had fallen from grace, of his governorship of Languedoc, for soon afterwards the other governors had their powers restored [7, XII *p. 779*].

The most complex and least efficient part of French government in the early sixteenth century was the fiscal administration [67; 121]. This was basically built around two kinds of royal revenue: the 'ordinary' revenue (*finances ordinaires**), which the king drew from his demesne and the 'extraordinary' revenue (*finances extraordinaires**) which he got from taxation. The 'extraordinary' revenue owed its name to the fact that originally it had been levied only for a special purpose and for a limited period, usually in wartime. By the sixteenth century, however, it consisted of regular taxes levied in times of peace and war. The 'ordinary' revenue comprised not only feudal rents, which were fixed and predictable, but also a wide range of variable dues owed to the king as suzerain.

The extraordinary revenue comprised three main taxes: the *taille**, the *gabelle** and the *aides**. The *taille* was the only direct tax [147]. It was levied annually, the amount being determined by the king's council, and it could be supplemented by a surtax (*crue**). There were two sorts of *taille*: the *taille reélle*, which was a land tax payable by all irrespective of social rank, and the *taille personnelle*, which fell mainly on land owned by unprivileged commoners. Of the two kinds of *taille*, the first was the fairer but it was found only in a few areas, notably Provence and Languedoc. The nobility and clergy were exempt from the *taille*, but it does not follow that the rest of society had to pay it. Many professional groups (e.g. royal officials, military personnel, municipal officials, lawyers, university teachers and students) were exempt. A large number of towns (*villes-franches**), including Paris, were also spared the tax. Thus, if the peasantry was *taillable*, the same was not true of all the bourgeoisie.

The *gabelle* was a tax on salt. By the late Middle Ages the salt trade had become so important in France that the Crown decided to share in its profits by controlling the sale and distribution of salt. But royal control was strongest in the northern and central provinces (*pays de grandes gabelles*), which had constituted the demesne of King Charles V (1364–80). Here, the salt was taken to royal warehouses (*greniers à sel**), where it was weighed and left to dry, usually for two years. It was then weighed again and taxed before the merchant who owned it was allowed to sell it. As a safeguard against illicit trading in salt, the Crown introduced the system of *sel par impôt*, whereby every household had to purchase from a royal *grenier* enough salt for its average needs. Outside the *pays de grandes gabelles* the salt tax was levied in different ways: in the west of France it was a quarter or a fifth of the sale price, while in the south a tariff was levied as the salt passed through royal warehouses situated along the coast near areas of production.

The *aides* were duties levied on various commodities sold regularly and in large quantities. The rate of tax was 1 *sou** per *livre* on all merchandise sold either wholesale or retail, except wine and other beverages which were taxed both ways. An important *aide* was the levy on livestock raised in many towns; another was the *aide* on wine, called *vingtième et huitième*. But indirect taxation, was, like the *taille*, subject to local variations; several parts of France were exempt from the *aides*.

How were taxes collected? The usual method in respect of the *taille* was for the leading men of the parish to elect from among themselves an assessor and a collector. The assessment, once completed, was read out in church by the local priest; a week later the parishioners paid their taxes to the collector as they left church. The assessor and collector were not inclined to leniency, for they were liable to be imprisoned or to have their own property confiscated if the sum collected fell short of the anticipated total. Indirect taxes were usually farmed by the highest bidder at an auction.

The most lucrative tax was the *taille*, which amounted to 2.4 million *livres* out of a total revenue of 4.9 million at the beginning of Francis I's reign. It was followed by the *aides*, which brought in about a third of the *taille*. As for the *gabelle*, it was bringing in 284,000 *livres* (about 6 per cent of the total revenue) in 1515.

The fiscal administration in 1515, like the tax system, had not changed since the reign of Charles VII (1422–61). It comprised two distinct administrations corresponding to the two kinds of revenue. The first (*Trésor*) was responsible for the 'ordinary' revenues. It was headed by four *trésoriers de France** with very wide powers. Each *trésorier* was in charge of one of four areas, called respectively Languedoïl, Languedoc, Normandy and Outre-Seine et Yonne. The *trésoriers* supervised the collection and disbursement of the revenues, but did not handle them; this task was left to subordinate officials (*receveurs ordinaires**), who were each responsible for a subdivision of the *bailliage*. The receiver-general for all revenues from the demesne was the *changeur du Trésor*. He was based in Paris, but only a small proportion of the revenues actually reached him, for the Crown settled many debts by means of warrants (*décharges**) assigned on a local treasurer. This avoided the expense and risk of transporting large amounts of cash along dangerous, bandit-infested roads, while passing on the recovery costs to the creditor.

The four *généraux des finances**, who had charge of the 'extraordinary' revenues, had virtually the same powers as the *trésoriers de France*, each being responsible for an area, called *généralité**. This was subdivided into *élections**, of which there were eighty-five at the start of the sixteenth century. But in general there were no *élections* in areas which retained their representative estates (*pays d'états**). The *élection* took its name from the *élu*, whose main function was to make regular tours of inspection (*chevauchées*) of his district, checking its ability to pay and the reliability of his underlings.

The personnel responsible for the administration of the *gabelles* varied in accordance with the different kinds of salt tax. In the *pays de grandes gabelles*, each *grenier* was under a *grenetier*, assisted by a *contrôleur*; elsewhere the tax was farmed out by commissioners.

On the same level as the *changeur du Trésor* and performing the same duties, though in respect of the 'extraordinary' revenues, were the four *receveurs généraux des finances*, one for each *généralité*.

The two fiscal administrations were not entirely separate, for the *trésoriers de France* and *généraux des finances* (known collectively as *gens des finances**) were expected to reside at court whenever they were not carrying out tours of inspection in their respective areas. They formed a financial committee, which met regularly and independently of the king's council, and were empowered to take certain decisions on their own. They also attended the king's council whenever important financial matters were discussed. However, their most important duty was to draw up at the start of each year a sort of national budget (*état général par estimation*), which was based on accounts sent in by each financial district.

PART TWO: ANALYSIS

3 THE MONARCHS: FRANCIS I AND HENRY II

The effectiveness of personal monarchy depended in the main on the age, health and lifespan of the monarch himself. In the first half of the sixteenth century the French monarchy was strong because it was in the hands of rulers who were adult, physically robust and reasonably long-lived. In spite of many accidents and illnesses, Francis I (1494–1547) died at the age of fifty-two, having ruled for thirty-two years (1515–47). His successor, Henry II (1519–59) was less fortunate: he was fatally injured in a tournament when only forty, having ruled for only twelve years (1547–59). France was then precipitated into the brief reign of the fifteen-year-old Francis II, followed by the minority of his brother, Charles IX, during which royal authority was seriously weakened.

During the troubles of the second half of the century Frenchmen looked back to the reign of Francis I with nostalgia. They called him 'the great king Francis', but later on the king's reputation declined. For Jules Michelet, the nineteenth-century French historian, Francis was anything but great. He summed up the king's career in two words: 'women' and 'war', or, as he put it, 'war to please women' [93, IX *pp. 344–6*]. And probably as a result of the influence exerted by Michelet on popular French historiography, Francis has until recently been given less serious attention than he deserves. His womanising and his liking for war are not to be denied, but his long reign marked a significant stage in the development of the French monarchy. It became more centralised than it had been in the late Middle Ages, and the reign witnessed two crucially important international movements: the Renaissance and the Reformation. Few reigns have left a more notable cultural and artistic legacy (see below pp. 76–81, 83–5).

Francis was born at Cognac on 12 September 1494. His father, Charles, count of Angoulême, belonged to a cadet branch of the house of Valois, while his mother, Louise, was the daughter of Philip, count of Bresse. At the time of his birth Francis seemed far removed from the throne: he was only the cousin of the reigning monarch, Charles VIII, and next in line to the throne was Louis, duke of Orleans. When Charles died childless in April 1498, Louis became Louis XII. In January 1499, having divorced his wife, Jeanne de France, who was barren, he married Charles VIII's widow, Anne of Brittany. She was only twenty-two years old and could reasonably be expected to produce a son, who would displace Francis as heir to the throne. But her only surviving children were daughters whom the Salic law* debarred from the succession. In 1514 Anne died and Louis XII took as his third wife, Mary Tudor, Henry VIII's beautiful sister, but he died soon afterwards and a rumour that he had left his young widow pregnant proved ill-founded. Thus it was more by luck than design that Francis reached the throne in January 1515 [21; 103].

Francis I was twenty-one years old at his accession and noted for his powerful physique. He was six feet tall with broad shoulders and muscular thighs, but below the knees his legs were thin and bandy (possibly the result of too much horse riding from an early age). His feet were long and flat. Although contemporaries praised Francis's good looks, modern taste may jib at his exceptionally long nose, a feature shared by his mother and sister. In temperament Francis was, it seems, very animated. Intelligent, quick-witted and eloquent, he displayed a keen interest in many subjects including hunting, ships, art and architecture. Although he had not had a classical education (he was never a good Latinist), he loved books and in the course of his reign built up one of the finest libraries in Europe, containing many rare classical manuscripts. Whenever he travelled about his kingdom, he carried with him chests filled with his favourite books, which were read to him aloud at meal times. They were mainly concerned with Roman history and the heroic deeds of antiquity. Francis was also quite a good poet, but he lacked the application necessary to scholarship. Essentially he was an outdoor type, who delighted in every kind of sport. Above all, he enjoyed hunting and devoted a substantial part of each day to it. He loved to shed cares of state and disappear into a forest, sometimes for several days, with a small band of companions. Foreign ambassadors were occasionally infuriated by the king's elusiveness, deeming it irresponsible, but the king could depend on able ministers. Ultimately, he was always in charge of affairs, even at the end of his reign, when his health was seriously undermined [*Doc. 16*]. Part of each morning was usually devoted to business, each afternoon to hunting, and each evening to dancing or some other courtly entertainment. Such a routine could, of course, be disrupted by war, which filled much of the reign. Francis's military campaigns in Italy and elsewhere revealed other strengths and flaws in his character. His bravery was demonstrated on many occasions, never more so than at the battle of Pavia, where he fought alone against overwhelming odds after his horse had been killed beneath him and most of his friends slaughtered. As the emperor's prisoner, he behaved with dignity and impressed his captors by his charm and affability. But where his interest was at stake, he could be deceitful. His repudiation of the peace of Madrid cannot be defended on moral grounds even if it was politically justified [*Doc. 6*]. Francis was also inclined to blame others for his own mistakes and could be ungrateful. Though generally humane, his harsh treatment of the elderly financier, Semblançay, who had done much to help him in the past, was a dark blot on his escutcheon [*Doc. 5*].

Among women who played an important role in Francis's life, three were outstanding: his mother, Louise of Savoy, his sister, Marguerite, and his first wife, Claude of France. After being widowed at nineteen, Louise was largely responsible for the education of her children. She devoted herself especially to her son's advancement, describing him as her 'Caesar' in her diary, and continued to serve him after his accession, twice as regent [79]. Her strong interest in foreign affairs earned her the description of 'mother and nourisher of peace' from Cardinal Wolsey [107 *p. 92*]. Her elder child, Marguerite, is best remembered for her literary works, notably her religious poems (e.g. *The Mirror of a Sinful Soul*) and her *Heptameron*, a collection of stories inspired by Boccaccio's *Decameron*. A strongly mystical outlook drew her to the teaching of Lefèvre d'Étaples and the *Cercle de Meaux*, and, after Protestantism had begun to make an impact on France, she tended to protect religious reformers and may have exercised a moderating influence on her brother's religious policy.

As for Queen Claude, she was no beauty, but became extremely popular on account of her sweet, charitable and pious nature. Within a period of nine years (she died in 1524) she bore her husband no less than three sons and four daughters. Of these children, only two, Henry and Marguerite, outlived their father. In 1530 Francis took as his second wife, Eleanor of Portugal, sister of his great rival, the emperor Charles V. The marriage had been a provision of the peace of Cambrai (1529) and as a purely political arrangement it was unlikely to yield much happiness to either party. Indeed, Eleanor seems to have been largely ignored by her husband, whose infidelities earned him a reputation for dissoluteness almost without equal. Among his many mistresses one deserves a special mention: Anne, duchess of Étampes, who became a powerful figure at the French court in the last ten years of the reign. She was a bitter enemy of the king's chief minister, Anne de Montmorency, and helped to bring about his dismissal in 1541 following the failure of his policy of reconciliation with the emperor. The artist, Benvenuto Cellini, whom she detested, has left a distinctly unflattering portrait of her in his *Autobiography* [10].

Under the terms of the treaty of Madrid (1526) [13, IV *p. 178*], Francis handed over two of his sons, François and Henry, to the emperor Charles V as hostages pending fulfilment of the treaty. The two boys (who were aged eight and seven respectively) spent four years as prisoners in Spain and their treatment was quite harsh, particularly after their father had defaulted on his obligations. One can only guess at the psychological effects on the children of this experience; it may perhaps explain the antipathy which developed between Henry and his father as well as Henry's undying hatred for Charles V. But an explanation of Henry's feelings for his father could be simply the jealousy commonly felt by a younger son for his elder brother, for the king began by reserving his affections for his eldest son. The untimely death of the dauphin François, probably from natural causes, in August 1536, did not lead to a transfer of the king's love to Henry. It passed instead to his third son, Charles, although Henry became the dauphin.

The last decade of Francis I's reign was marked by a bitter rivalry between his two remaining sons. The rift between them widened in 1541 following the fall of Montmorency. While Henry remained loyal to the minister throughout his disgrace, Charles became the darling of the duchess of Étampes. Each prince became the focus of a party at court: while Montmorency's friends rallied round Henry, his enemies gathered round Charles. The rivalry between the brothers was exacerbated by their military performance in the war of 1542: whereas Charles acquired glory by conquering Luxemburg, Henry was forced to retreat from Perpignan. An even worse blow to Henry was the peace of Crépy (1544), which was designed to advance his brother's prospects at the expense of his own interests. This threat, however, was removed in September 1545, when Charles died of plague. Thereafter the king drew closer to the dauphin, but the old wounds were not easily healed.

The death of Francis I (31 March 1547) was followed immediately by a palace revolution [*Doc. 17*]. The new king, Henry II, began by cleaning up the court. He curbed its entertainments so as to devote more time to 'grave and virtuous thoughts' and cashiered Francis's 'fair band of ladies'. Madame d'Étampes was forced to disgorge the jewels given to her by Francis and banished to one of her country houses. Into her shoes stepped her arch-enemy, Diane de Poitiers. As Henry's mistress (she was forty-eight and he only twenty-seven!), she now became the dominant woman at court, receiving gifts and dispensing favours to her favourites and kinsmen. Even more important was the return to power of Montmorency, who had been living in retirement since 1541 [*Doc. 18*]. In July 1551 he was created a duke and a peer, an unprecedented elevation for a mere baron, placing him on a par with the highest in the land. His rehabilitation automatically entailed the disgrace of Admiral Annebault and Cardinal Tournon, who had run the government in Francis I's last years. The most sinister aspect of the palace revolution was the ascendancy of the house of Guise represented by François, comte d'Aumale (soon to be duke), and Charles, archbishop of Rheims (soon to be cardinal). Both were in the flower of manhood, intelligent and immensely ambitious [104, I].

Historians have, on the whole, done less than justice to Henry II [*Doc. 22*]. He has been portrayed by Michelet as a gloomy monarch. Yet, after his accession, he shed the melancholia that had marked his unhappy youth [104, I]. In 1547 a Venetian envoy described him as 'joyful, rubicund and with an excellent colour'. He was fond of practical jokes and, being tall and muscular like his father, loved all sports, particularly tennis, riding and jousting. Intellectually, however, he was less sharp than his father: literary pursuits and the fine arts bored him. His private life was only a shade more respectable than Francis's. He shared it with his wife, Catherine de' Medici (who after ten childless years of marriage miraculously produced four sons and three daughters in eleven years), and his mistress, Diane [43]. But the king also had a number of affairs on the side (e.g. with Lady Fleming) which produced illegimate children.

Henry's faults and qualities were fairly evenly balanced. He was kind to his offspring and loyal to his friends (especially those who had stood by him under Francis), but he was vindictive and stubborn. In the exercise of his kingly duties, Henry was reasonably conscientious and hard-working. He lacked experience, having been excluded from public affairs by his father, and tended to rely heavily on people he trusted. According to the Ferrarese ambassador, Henry trembled whenever Montmorency appeared 'as children do when they see their teacher'. Yet the king was not spineless: at council meetings and in diplomatic audiences, he listened attentively and spoke clearly and sensibly. But it is difficult for the historian to disentangle the king's ideas from those of his ministers. It seems that the recovery of Calais mattered far more to him than the realisation of French claims in Italy. His court, however, was filled with Italians, and French policy did to some extent reflect their personal ambitions and enthusiasms. Thus Henry pressed on with the conquest of Piedmont and planned to revive the Angevin claim to Naples in the interest of one of his sons. Such long-term aims, however, were frustrated by the king's tragic end: on 30 June 1559 he was fatally wounded in a tournament held in Paris to celebrate the peace of Cateau-Cambrésis. He died in great pain on 10 July [*Doc. 21*]. His heir, Francis II, was only fifteen years old. Under French law he was old enough to be king, but in practice the government passed into the hands of the Guises. The scene was set for the bloody struggle for power in the course of which the monarchy of Renaissance France all but collapsed.

4 FOREIGN AFFAIRS

THE ITALIAN WARS

The great powers of western Europe – France and the Holy Roman Empire – were usually at war during the first half of the sixteenth century and their main area of conflict was Italy. The explanation often given for this state of affairs is that France wanted to break out of her encirclement by territories ruled by the house of Habsburg, but the evidence is against this. France was not really 'encircled' until the Spanish ruler, Charles of Habsburg, was elected Holy Roman Emperor in 1519 [*Doc. 4*], yet the Italian wars had begun in 1494. What is more, French foreign policy in the early sixteenth century was concerned with the assertion of dynastic rights, not with the achievement of 'natural frontiers'. The French kings intervened in Italy because they claimed a legal right to certain parts of the peninsula, particularly the duchy of Milan and the kingdom of Naples.

Italy at this time was a tempting prey to a relatively large and united neighbour, for it consisted of several more or less independent states, which could be easily played off against each other. The most important were the republic of Venice, which, in addition to an extensive territory, held lands along the Adriatic's eastern seaboard, in the Aegean and in the eastern Mediterranean; the duchy of Milan, which was ruled by the house of Sforza; the republic of Florence under the effective authority of the Medici family; the States of the Church, stretching diagonally across the peninsula from the Tiber to the Po and ruled by the pope; and the kingdom of Naples, the only feudal monarchy, which was divided into two parts – Sicily and the mainland – and ruled by branches of the house of Aragon. Notable among the lesser Italian states were the duchy of Savoy, sitting astride the Alps, the republic of Genoa and the duchy of Ferrara.

Peace was more or less maintained in Italy by a policy of equilibrium among the principal states, but this was upset in 1494 by the armed intervention of King Charles VIII of France, who founded his ambitions on earlier French successes in the peninsula: the house of Anjou had once ruled Naples and that of Orleans had intermarried with the Visconti, who had ruled Milan before the Sforza. The French invasion precipitated a revolution in Florence and the overthrow of the Medici. Naples fell into French hands, but the formation of a coalition against Charles forced him to return home in haste. He narrowly escaped defeat at Fornovo. In 1499 his successor, Louis XII, captured Milan and Genoa, but unwisely agreed to partition Naples with the wily Ferdinand of Aragon. Conflict soon broke out between the partners, and in 1504 the whole of Naples passed under the Aragonese crown. Four years later Louis joined a coalition against Venice engineered by Pope Julius II. Once Venice had been defeated, however, the pope devoted all his energies to expelling the French from the peninsula. With the military aid of the Swiss (then the best mercenary troops in Europe) he achieved his purpose. An attempt by Louis to stage a comeback in 1513 ended disastrously: the Swiss, after routing his army at Novara, swept into Burgundy and besieged Dijon. They withdrew only after the local commander had signed a humiliating treaty which Louis subsequently refused to ratify [22; 103].

By January 1515 France had lost all her Italian territories. The Sforza had been restored to power in Milan in the person of Massimiliano Sforza, Genoa was independent and the whole of Naples belonged to Aragon. A twofold responsibility thus weighed upon Francis I at the start of his reign: he was expected to regain the ground lost by his predecessors and to avenge the defeats suffered by French arms. His youthful spirit and powerful physique fitted him well for the task. Francis immediately set about neutralising his more powerful neighbours. He signed treaties with the fifteen-year-old Archduke Charles (the future Emperor Charles V), who ruled the Low Countries and Franche-Comté, and with King Henry VIII of England. In Italy, however, Francis's diplomacy was less successful. The Venetians agreed to help him in return for aid against emperor Maximilian, and the Genoese reverted to their former allegiance to France in exchange for local concessions. But the other powers showed no inclination to co-operate with France. In July 1515 Sforza, Pope Leo X, Ferdinand of Aragon and the emperor Maximilian formed a league to defend Italy.

After appointing his mother, Louise of Savoy, as regent, Francis led his army across the Alps in August 1515. Using a little-known pass, he managed to elude the Swiss who had been guarding the main approaches to Milan. But the city would not admit him, so that he was forced to pitch camp just outside, at Marignano. On 13 September the Swiss came out of Milan and attacked the king's camp only to be heavily defeated in a long and bloody encounter [80]. A veteran of the Italian Wars, Marshal Trivulzio, described it as a 'battle of giants' beside which others he had witnessed seemed like 'children's games'. The immediate results of the battle were the French capture of Milan and the overthrow of Sforza, who retired to France on a pension.

No one was more disturbed by this outcome than Pope Leo X, who had backed the wrong horse. He was afraid that Francis would follow up his victory by marching on Florence and toppling his Medici relatives. But Leo had nothing to fear. Recent history had shown that France could only establish a lasting foothold in Italy with papal co-operation. Moreover, the threat of a possible Anglo-imperial coalition prompted Francis to seek the pope's support or at least to neutralise him [136]. In December he and the pope met in Bologna and agreed to co-operate in various ways. Their most important decision – the substitution of a Concordat for the Pragmatic Sanction of Bourges of 1438 – legalised and enlarged royal control of the Church in France [*Doc. 2*].

The death of Ferdinand of Aragon in January 1516 altered the balance of power in Europe. His grandson, the archduke Charles, who already ruled the Low Countries and Franche-Comté, suddenly acquired the kingdoms of Castile, Aragon and Naples. He became overnight France's most powerful neighbour and the ruler of territories in which she had an interest [33]. Francis had inherited a claim to Naples, which its suzerain, the pope, seemed ready to support. Another potential trouble spot was Spanish Navarre, which Ferdinand had wrested from its king, Jean d'Albret, in 1512. As duke of Burgundy, Charles had implicitly recognised Albret's claim, but he was unlikely to do so as king of Spain. Nor was he likely to give up Naples, which had become an integral part of the Spanish empire in the Mediterranean. These, however, were but storm clouds on the horizon. For the time being, Charles had to remain on amicable terms with Francis, for he still had to take up possession of his Spanish kingdoms and there were powerful forces within Aragon and Castile favouring a return to separate rulers. In August, therefore, Charles signed the treaty of Noyon with Francis [13, I *p. 409*]. He was to marry Francis's daughter, Louise, who was to receive Naples as her dowry. Pending completion of the marriage, Charles promised to pay Francis an annual tribute for Naples, thereby implicitly recognising the French claim. The treaty enabled Charles to establish his authority in Spain without French interference and Francis to consolidate his position in Italy.

In March 1516 an attempt by the emperor Maximilian to dislodge the French from Milan ended in fiasco: he waited two days outside the city, then suddenly decamped, leaving his troops in the lurch. His ignominious flight helped Francis to reach a settlement with the Swiss. In the so-called 'perpetual peace' of Fribourg (November 1516) they undertook, in return for a pension, to serve no one against the king. In future, he would be able to hire Swiss mercenaries instead of fighting them. In March 1517 Francis, Maximilian and Charles of Spain agreed at Cambrai to help each other, if attacked, and to join forces in a crusade. This rounded off the first phase of the Italian Wars and Francis could feel reasonably satisfied with the results so far of his foreign policy: he had shown his martial valour, avenged the disasters of 1513 and exploded the myth of Swiss invincibility. The emperor had been made to look absurd in European eyes, Milan and Genoa had reverted to French rule and the pope seemed subservient.

Peace came at a time when Christendom desperately needed to unite against the westward expansion of the Ottoman Turks. Under Mehmet II they had captured Constantinople (1453) and penetrated far into the Balkans. Now, under Selim the Grim, they were again advancing: after conquering Syria (1516), they invaded Egypt. In March 1518 the pope proclaimed a Christian truce and dispatched nuncios to the principal courts so as to rally support for a crusade. But no one was really interested. Although the seriousness of the Turkish threat was generally recognised, other problems seemed more urgent to the secular rulers of Christendom.

VALOIS–HABSBURG RIVALRY

Now that Charles of Habsburg had taken possession of his Spanish kingdoms, the treaty of Noyon was a millstone round his neck. He could not afford the tribute for Naples and showed no inclination to compensate the house of Albret for its loss of Spanish Navarre. In May 1519 a conference was held at Montpellier to sort out differences between Francis and Charles, but it got off to a bad start, and the sudden death of Boisy, the chief French negotiator, hastened its collapse. Meanwhile, the death in January of the emperor Maximilian threw open the contest for the Holy Roman Empire.

Although the Empire had for long been in Habsburg hands, it was an elective, not a hereditary, dignity: the emperor was chosen by seven electors – the archbishops of Mainz, Cologne and Trier, the king of Bohemia, the elector-palatine, the duke of Saxony and the margrave of Brandenburg. They were not compelled to choose a Habsburg or even a German. Indeed, as early as 1516, the archbishops of Trier and Mainz had offered to vote for Francis at the next election, and they were soon joined by the margrave and the elector-palatine. The empire attracted Francis on two counts: first, it was a supranational dignity – the secular counterpart of the papacy – and had, therefore, great international prestige. Secondly, Francis knew that Maximilian wanted to be succeeded by his grandson Charles, who already ruled the Low Countries, Franche-Comté, Spain and Naples. If he were to become emperor, he would be indisputably the most powerful ruler in Christendom. As suzerain of Milan, he might try to wrest the duchy from Francis, and, should he go to Italy to be crowned emperor by the pope, he might be tempted to drive the French out of the peninsula. By offering himself as a candidate Francis hoped to avert these dangers.

What Francis failed to see was that the German electors were interested less in his success than in promoting a contested election, which would offer them marvellous opportunities for bribery and corruption. Thus, after they had offered to vote for Francis, a majority of the electors promised Maximilian, in return for bribes, to support his grandson. Then, following the emperor's death, they invited new bids from the rival candidates. Francis spent a huge sum (400,000 crowns) trying to win them over, but he was denied exchange facilities by the German bankers, notably the Fuggers of Augsburg, whose own long-term interests were best served by supporting the Habsburgs [108]. German public opinion was also strongly hostile to the French candidate. He was portrayed by Habsburg agents as a tyrant, who mercilessly fleeced his subjects. On 28 June 1519 Charles was elected unanimously [*Doc. 4*].

One result of the imperial election was to enhance England's international standing. Whereas previously there had been four major powers in Europe – France, Spain, the Empire and England – now there were only three, Spain and the Empire having become united in the person of Charles. Of these France and the Empire seemed of roughly equal weight so that England found herself in an influential position: 'her alliance would bestow dominance, while her neutrality could, in theory, guarantee peace' [107 *p. 81*]. It was in pursuit of this 'policy of imbalance' that Cardinal Wolsey, Henry

VIII's chief minister, revived an idea mooted in the treaty of London (October 1518) for a meeting between Henry and Francis. This took place near Calais in June 1520 and is justly famous as the Field of Cloth of Gold [105]. It has been called by A.F. Pollard 'perhaps the most portentous deception on record', yet the Anglo-imperial agreement which immediately followed it was not necessarily a betrayal of Francis. Wolsey hoped to impose a Christian peace by holding the balance between Francis and Charles, but this depended less on England's neutrality than on the willingness of her two powerful neighbours to sink their differences.

The uneasy peace of Christendom was broken in 1521 when Charles and Francis accused each other of making war. The aggressor was certainly Francis, though it may be doubted whether he wanted a full-scale conflict. His main purpose was to keep Charles out of Italy by stirring up trouble for him in Luxemburg and Navarre. Where Francis had miscalculated was in assuming that Charles would not react vigorously. In April an imperial army under Henry of Nassau threatened France's northern border. By the summer Francis had cause to regret his provocations. He accepted an offer of arbitration from Henry and a conference met at Calais under Wolsey's chairmanship, but the emperor was in no mood to compromise [132; 144]. While the talks were still in progress, his army invaded north-east France and laid siege to Mézières. Meanwhile, Pope Leo X abandoned his friendship with France, which had brought him nothing but irritation, and allied with Charles. In November the imperialists, under Prospero Colonna, launched an offensive in north Italy, capturing Milan. About the same time, the Calais conference collapsed, and England, acting on a treaty signed secretly at Bruges, entered the war on the imperial side. In March 1522 Marshal Lautrec, who commanded the French army in north Italy, tried to recapture Milan, only to be decisively crushed at La Bicocca (27 April). Soon the French had lost everything in Italy, save the castles of Milan and Cremona [*Doc. 5*].

In July 1523 Francis left Paris with the intention of leading a new invasion of Italy, but on his way south to join his army he received a warning that his chief vassal, Charles of Bourbon, constable of France, was plotting treason. Soon afterwards Bourbon went over to the emperor, leaving his accomplices to be rounded up in France. These dramatic events threw the king's plans into disarray. While he remained in France, the Italian invasion was entrusted to his favourite, Admiral Bonnivet, who, in April 1524, was resoundingly defeated by the viceroy of Naples. This disaster was followed in July by an imperial invasion of Provence led by the traitor Bourbon, which ought to have coincided with an English invasion of northern France. But Henry VIII, under the influence of Wolsey who was rightly sceptical of Bourbon's chances of success, failed to provide the necessary support. Marseilles also proved an insurmountable obstacle in the duke's path. After besieging the city for more than a month, he decided in late September to retreat into Italy [80]. The fighting season was virtually over, yet Francis snatched at the chance of carrying out his long-deferred plan. He led his army across the Alps in record time and entered Milan by one gate as the imperialists left by another. But he then made the fatal mistake of besieging Pavia, thereby committing his troops to a harsh winter in the open. After much skirmishing on both sides, the imperialists forced a pitched battle (24 February 1525) which ended in Francis's defeat and capture [80]. Among the large number of dead on the French side were many of his closest friends and advisers. It was the worst slaughter of French nobles since Agincourt. For more than a year Francis was the emperor's prisoner, first in a castle near Cremona, then in Spain. Eventually he secured his release by promising, in the treaty of Madrid, to hand over the duchy of Burgundy to Charles and by surrendering two of his sons as hostages [13, IV *p. 178*]. Meanwhile, his mother, Louise of Savoy, who administered France in his absence, saved his kingdom from invasion by skilfully detaching Henry VIII from his alliance with the emperor (treaty of the More, August 1525) [13, IV *p. 92*].

No sooner had Francis regained his freedom than he refused to ratify the peace of Madrid on the ground that he had signed it under duress [*Doc. 6*]. Instead of ceding Burgundy, he offered the emperor a ransom in cash. In May 1526 he joined the Holy League of Cognac, a grouping of Italian states designed to expel the emperor from the peninsula, but he wanted to use the league to put pressure on Charles rather than actively to join in a military enterprise. As a result, his Italian allies, who confidently believed that the hour of their independence had struck, found him less than wholehearted in supporting their cause. Pope Clement VII, in particular, became thoroughly disgruntled and signed a truce with the viceroy of Naples. This, however, failed to avert the sack of Rome (May 1527) by an imperial army led by Bourbon. An immediate consequence of this event, which left the pope virtually the emperor's prisoner, was a *rapprochement* between England and France, which found expression in the treaty of Amiens (August 1527) [13, V *p. 87*].

The pope's plight gave Francis an excuse for a new military intervention south of the Alps. In August an army under Marshal Lautrec overran Lombardy except Milan, while the Genoese admiral, Andrea Doria, who had entered the service of France, captured Genoa. This ended any prospect of a peaceful settlement of the differences between Francis and Charles. The latter refused to release Francis's sons at any price as long as the French army remained in Italy. In January 1528 England and France declared war on him and in April Lautrec laid siege to Naples. No one expected the city to hold out for long, as it was also being blockaded from the sea by a fleet commanded by Doria's nephew, Filippino. However, Doria's disenchantment with his French employer suddenly changed the situation. Early in July, Filippino, acting on his uncle's orders, removed his fleet from the bay of Naples so that supplies were soon able to reach the city. This was followed by an outbreak of cholera or plague in the French camp, which carried off Lautrec and a large proportion of his army. The survivors soon capitulated. In 1529 another French army under Saint-Pol was crushed at Landriano as it tried to recapture Genoa, which had recently regained its independence. The French collapse convinced the pope, who by now had been set free, that he had nothing to gain by staying neutral. In June 1529 he signed the treaty of Barcelona in which he promised to crown Charles emperor and to absolve all those responsible for the sack of Rome.

In July 1529 peace talks took place at Cambrai between Louise of Savoy, acting for her son, and Louise's sister-in-law, Margaret of Savoy, acting for her nephew, the emperor. They resulted in the 'peace of the ladies' (3 August), which in all essentials was a revision of the peace of Madrid [13, V *p. 221*]. In place of Burgundy, Charles accepted a ransom of 2 million gold crowns. Francis gave up his Italian claims, various towns in northern France and his suzerainty over Flanders and Artois. His Italian allies were left out of the treaty and Henry VIII was only accommodated at the eleventh hour. Charles, for his part, promised to send his sister Eleanor whose marriage to Francis had been laid down by the peace of Madrid; he also released Francis's sons. Humiliating as it was for France, the peace of Cambrai was less disastrous for her than historians have often supposed, for in two important respects it vindicated Francis's diplomacy since 1526: he kept Burgundy and recovered his sons for a cash ransom. From the emperor's standpoint the peace was opportune, since it enabled him to settle the affairs of Italy before attending to the grave problems presented by the Lutheran Reformation in Germany. On 24 February 1530 he was crowned emperor by Pope Clement VII in Bologna.

The peace entailed no fundamental change in French foreign policy. It merely provided Francis with a breathing-space in which to replenish his treasury, rebuild his forces and consolidate his alliances. Between 1530 and 1534 he stirred up trouble for the emperor in Germany and in the Mediterranean without openly contravening the recent peace treaty. The election in January 1531 of Charles's brother, Ferdinand, as King of the Romans helped to widen the rift between the emperor and many German princes. Protestants among them were alarmed by the election of a Catholic ruler dedicated to the preservation of his faith. They appealed to Francis for help, and in February six Protestant princes and ten cities formed the Schmalkaldic league to defend their interests. Although Francis had undertaken at Cambrai not to meddle in German affairs, he found the princes' appeal irresistible. In May 1532, therefore, he promised them a subsidy to help them reconquer Württemberg from the Habsburgs. In the same year, he and Henry VIII met for the second time at Boulogne. Though ostensibly directed against the Turks, their meeting was really aimed at co-ordinating their actions in Germany and in Rome. While Francis wanted Henry to share the burden of subsidising the German princes, Henry needed French support for his divorce. Having recently got rid of Wolsey, the only English cardinal, he now depended on French cardinals to manipulate the Curia. His impatience, however, frustrated French efforts on his behalf. By marrying Anne Boleyn in secret, Henry ensured that sooner or later he would be excommunicated by the pope. Francis was able only to delay this eventuality for as long as possible. In March 1534 Clement fulminated his anathema against the king of England who responded by completing England's breach with Rome.

Francis, meanwhile, met the pope at Marseilles (October 1533) and discussed various topics with him, including the spread of heresy and the calling of a general council of the Church. The main result of the meeting, however, was the marriage of the king's second son, Henry, duke of Orleans, with the pope's niece, Catherine de' Medici [43]. It is possible that this was the outward manifestation of a new Franco-papal alliance aimed at causing trouble for the emperor in Italy, but this was never formalised in a treaty. What is certain is that Francis continued meddling in German affairs. While his agent, Guillaume du Bellay, tried to heal the religious schism among the German princes which stood in the way of a united opposition to the Habsburgs, the king himself met the landgrave of Hesse at Bar-le-Duc in January 1534 and signed a treaty with him [32]. Soon afterwards, the landgrave overran Württemberg, restoring its duke, whom the Habsburgs had deposed. Francis's intrigues also extended to the Mediterranean, where he negotiated with Khair-ad-Din Barbarossa, an Algerian corsair employed by the Ottoman sultan [116]. In August, Barbarossa captured Tunis, expelling its ruler, Muley Hassan, who was the emperor's ally. This action prompted Charles to mount an expedition against Barbarossa.

During the second half of 1534 two major events radically altered the international situation. The first was the death of Pope Clement VII, in September, and the subsequent election of Alessandro Farnese as Pope Paul III. This automatically removed the political significance of the recent marriage between the duke of Orleans and Catherine de' Medici, reducing it to the status of a *mésalliance*. The second was the Affair of the Placards (see pages 65–6), an act of defiance by a group of French Protestant radicals which provoked a savage campaign of religious persecution in France [*Doc. 11*]. Protestant opinion throughout Europe was shocked and imperial agents in Germany successfully undermined Francis's credibility among his Protestant allies by pointing to the shameful contrast between his cruel treatment of their French co-religionists and his friendly dealings with the Infidel Turk.

Charles V's war preparations against the Barbary corsairs of north Africa provided Francis with a new *casus belli*. 'If the emperor arms', he declared, 'I cannot but do the same.' As he toured northern France reviewing his newly established provincial legions, his diplomats were active in every corner of Europe. In February 1536, for example, Jean de la Forêt negotiated at Constantinople with Ibrahim, the sultan's chief minister, and they almost certainly reached an agreement on military co-operation. Another important envoy was Jean du Bellay, who went to Italy in June 1535, mainly to win over Paul III and to dissuade him from calling a general council, which Francis believed would only serve to increase the emperor's power.

In spite of the warlike noises coming from the French court and the intrigues of French diplomats everywhere, Charles pressed on with his own war plan. In June 1535 he sailed out of Barcelona at the head of a large expeditionary force and soon afterwards captured Tunis. On 22 August he landed in Sicily at the start of a triumphal progress that was to take him up the whole length of

Italy. Francis in the meantime, did nothing, much to the chagrin of the warmongers at his court, led by Admiral Chabot. Montmorency had given his word to the imperial ambassador that the king would not take unfair advantage of Charles's absence, but probably the main reason for the king's inertia was his lack of preparedness. By the time he was ready to move, the fighting season was almost over.

In November 1535 the question of the Milanese succession was reopened, when Francesco Sforza, who had ruled the duchy since 1525, died without leaving a male heir. Francis at once claimed the duchy for his second son, Henry of Orleans, but this was unacceptable to the emperor, for Henry was too close to the French throne. Charles, however, did not rule out the possibility of Milan being given to Francis's third son, Charles, duke of Angoulême. Matters stood thus in January 1536, when Francis suddenly invaded the duchy of Savoy. He declared that he was only seeking to recover lands which its ruler, Charles III, had wrongfully annexed. But this was only a transparent excuse for an act of naked aggression aimed at providing Francis with a useful bargaining counter in his negotiations with the emperor over Milan's future. The French invasion of Savoy, however, caused great offence to the emperor, who was the duke's brother-in-law and ally. He was too remote at first to come to the duke's aid, but on reaching Rome in April he denounced Francis's action in a speech before the pope and Sacred College [33].

By May 1536 an undeclared state of war existed between France and the Empire. As the imperialists marched into Piedmont, the marquis of Saluzzo, who led the French forces, defected to the enemy. This seriously weakened the French hold on Piedmont, but, instead of attempting their expulsion, Charles V invaded Provence on 24 July. Montmorency, who defended the province, wisely opted for a strictly defensive strategy: leaving Aix to its fate, he created a vacuum in front of the advancing enemy by a policy of 'scorched earth'. After capturing Aix, the provincial capital, the emperor found himself in the same predicament as Bourbon in 1524. Marseilles stood in his path. As he pondered over his next move, the combination of hot weather, poor sanitation and inadequate supplies caused havoc in his camp. By 2 September he had allegedly lost 8,000 men through famine or disease. Nine days later he ordered a retreat. Meanwhile, in northern France, his lieutenant, Henry of Nassau, made an unsuccessful bid to capture Péronne.

In July 1537 the fighting in northern France was brought to an end by the truce of Bomy. This enabled Francis to mount a rescue operation for his troops in Italy. Montmorency crossed the Alps in October and, forcing his way along the Val di Susa, relieved several garrisons in Piedmont. By now, however, both sides felt exhausted. A truce was accordingly signed at Monzón (16 November), which was followed by peace talks at Leucate, but they broke down over the Milanese question. This disappointed Montmorency, who favoured a reconciliation between his master and the emperor. His personal achievement, however, was unaffected: in February 1538 he was rewarded for his victory in Provence with the office of constable of France which had remained vacant since Bourbon's treason [50, I].

French foreign policy turned a somersault in 1538: after years of bitter hostility towards the emperor, Francis suddenly became his friend. The instigator of this extraordinary *volte-face* was Paul III, who saw peace in Christendom as the essential prerequisite to a general council or a crusade against the Turks. His efforts to turn the existing truce into a lasting peace culminated in a meeting at Nice (May and June 1538) between himself, Francis and Charles. The king and the emperor refused to meet each other, even in the pope's presence, and in the end, Paul had to be content with a new ten-year truce. Yet Franco-imperial contacts were established during the meeting which resulted, on 14 July, in a memorable encounter between Francis and Charles at Aigues-Mortes in Languedoc. Warm greetings and tokens of brotherly love were exchanged by them, and soon afterwards, Charles accepted in principle certain marriage proposals submitted by Francis. Although many people, including the pope, viewed the reconciliation with scepticism, Montmorency at least took it seriously. Under his direction the French government honoured the new entente, hoping that Charles would reciprocate by eventually handing over Milan. The ultimate objective of French foreign policy remained unchanged; only its method was now different. Francis abstained from any new involvement in Germany's domestic affairs and offered to mediate between Charles and the sultan. In the winter of 1539–40 he invited the emperor, who was faced by a revolt in Ghent, to travel across France on his way from Spain to the Low Countries. But, after enjoying Francis's magnificent hospitality, Charles failed to produce any satisfactory offer regarding Milan. In October 1540 he even invested his son, Philip, with the duchy, thereby precipitating Montmorency's disgrace. As the constable ceased to control French foreign policy, the king reverted to his traditional ways.

In July 1541 Franco-imperial relations were further damaged

following the murder of two French diplomats by imperial troops in Lombardy. Francis interpreted this crime and the emperor's descent into Italy soon afterwards as the opening moves of a campaign aimed at ousting the French from Piedmont. In fact, Charles was preparing a new expedition against the Infidel in north Africa, which took place in the autumn and ended in failure outside Algiers. Even so Francis declared war on Charles on 12 July 1542 and launched a twofold offensive against Luxemburg in the north and Perpignan in the south; but it soon petered out. Diplomatically the war caused a revival of the Anglo-imperial alliance. Relations between Francis and Henry VIII had been cooling for some time: Henry complained that Francis had defaulted on his pension and other obligations due under past treaties. Maritime disputes and Scotland were among other sources of friction. In June 1543 the king of England and the emperor declared war on France, but it was in the Mediterranean that the most startling developments took place. After the combined French and Turkish fleets had captured Nice in August, Francis placed the port of Toulon at the disposal of his ally, Barbarossa. Christendom was stunned by the transformation of a Christian town into a Muslim one, complete with mosque and slave-market! Even Francis had doubts about the arrangement, and he was clearly relieved when Barbarossa and his fleet left in May 1544.

During the summer of 1544 Charles V and Henry VIII both invaded northern France in person: while the emperor besieged Saint-Dizier, the king attacked Montreuil and Boulogne. At first, Charles made good progress, but Saint-Dizier proved a tougher nut to crack than expected. By holding out for forty-one days, the town broke the impetus of the imperial invasion. On 11 September Charles ordered a retreat. Francis, meanwhile, put out unofficial peace-feelers in the hope of detaching one of the parties to the Anglo-imperial coalition. Henry would listen to no overtures until he had captured Boulogne, an objective that was not achieved till 13 September. But Charles was anxious to pull out of the war so as to be free to deal with the religious situation in Germany. On 18 September he and Francis signed the peace of Crépy, whose main proposal was for a marriage between Charles duke of Orleans and either Charles's daughter, Maria, or his niece, Anna. In the first case the duke was to receive the Low Countries and Franche-Comté as dowry; in the second, Milan.

Not every Frenchman liked the peace (the dauphin Henry protested against it formally), but it was soon a dead letter, for

Charles of Orleans died in September 1545. Meanwhile, Anglo-French peace talks at Calais foundered on Henry VIII's refusal to hand back Boulogne and on his insistence that France should abandon the Scots. Since a negotiated settlement seemed impossible, the French tried to force Henry into a more reasonable attitude by an attack on the south coast of England. In July 1545 French troops landed in the Isle of Wight and at Seaford (Sussex), but they did little damage and soon withdrew. An attack by the Scots along England's northern border also proved abortive. By early September, the war had reached a stalemate. Within a short time, therefore, new peace talks were under way which resulted in the treaty of Ardres (7 June 1546) in which France agreed to pay 2 million crowns in 1554 for the return of Boulogne.

The accession of Henry II to the French throne in March 1547 and the return to power of the constable of Montmorency produced no startling change in French foreign policy. While the constable and his Châtillon nephews favoured peace, the rival faction of Guise (led by François, duke of Aumale and his brother Charles, cardinal of Lorraine) pressed for a resumption of war with England. In 1548 the Guises cut across English designs in Scotland by carrying off their niece, Mary Stuart, and marrying her to Henry II's eldest son, the dauphin Francis. In August 1549 Henry II declared war on England and invaded the Boulogne region in person. The conflict, however, was short-lived. In October, the protector Somerset was overthrown and replaced as Edward VI's chief minister by the earl of Warwick, whose first serious move in foreign policy was to make peace with France. She recovered Boulogne for a much smaller sum than that fixed in 1546.

Having made peace with England, Henry, who had never forgiven Charles V for his long detention in Spain as a hostage after the peace of Madrid, felt free to direct his attention to the Empire. Early in 1550 the German Protestants began talks with the king which culminated in the treaty of Chambord (15 January 1552). In return for a subsidy, Henry was empowered to occupy the towns of Cambrai, Metz, Toul and Verdun as 'imperial vicar'. By then, war between France and the Empire had already begun, but it was only in April 1552 that Henry embarked on a campaign known to contemporaries as 'the German voyage' [123, I]. It began with Montmorency's capture of Metz and Henry's occupation of Lorraine. Early in May, after crossing the Vosges mountains, the king's army gathered in the Alsatian plain. Passing close to Strassburg, he occupied Haguenau, but, on learning that the

German Protestant leader, Maurice of Saxony, had come to terms with the King of the Romans, Henry halted his advance. Retreating westward, he entered Verdun and in late July disbanded his army. The emperor meanwhile drew closer to the German Protestants, and at the diet of Passau reached a settlement with them which freed him for action against his foreign enemies. In the autumn of 1552 he besieged Metz, but met his match in François, duke of Guise, who defended the town. As the weeks elapsed the imperial army began to succumb to the hardships of a severe winter in the open. By 2 January 1553, when Charles lifted the siege, his army had dwindled to a third of its original size.

If the emperor failed at Metz, he scored a major diplomatic triumph in July 1554 by marrying his son, Philip, to the English queen, Mary Tudor. His aim, however, was not to drag England into the war, at least not immediately, for Charles, at fifty-five, was an old man by sixteenth-century standards and in poor health. He wanted peace in order to abdicate. In October 1555 at a touching ceremony in Brussels he resigned his rule in the Low Countries to Philip and in January 1556 he also handed over his Spanish and Italian kingdoms. The Holy Roman Empire passed to his brother, Ferdinand. Charles then retired to a monastery in Castile, where he died in September 1558.

The abdication of Charles V was followed almost at once by the truce of Vaucelles between his government and France. It was intended to last five years, but was soon broken, largely because of the intrigues of the new pope, Paul IV, and his nephew, Cardinal Carlo Carafa. Paul hated the Spaniards on account of their occupation of his native Naples, and he looked to France for help in driving them out. The pope could rely on the support of the Guise faction at the French court, but not on that of Montmorency, whose influence with Henry II was uppermost at this time. However, Carafa as legate worked strenuously to bring France round to the papal view, while Paul provoked Philip II of Spain by acts of aggression along the Neapolitan border. In September 1556 the duke of Alba, viceroy of Naples, invaded the States of the Church, whereupon Henry sent the duke of Guise to Italy with a strong army. Ostensibly, the purpose of this expedition was to aid the pope; in reality it was to conquer Naples [104, II]. For Henry had not given up his father's Italian ambitions. Historians who have suggested that the king's 'German voyage' marked a radical change in French foreign policy away from Italy and in favour of pushing France's eastern border to the Rhine are wrong: Henry was incapable of innovation and there was no demand among contemporary Frenchmen for a Rhine frontier [123, I].

Yet it was in northern France, not Italy, that the outcome of the war was decided. In August 1557 a Spanish army, commanded by Emmanuel-Philibert, the exiled duke of Savoy, invaded northern France from the Low Countries and laid siege to Saint-Quentin. Montmorency went to the town's relief but moved so slowly and clumsily that he was heavily defeated (10 August) and taken prisoner. His removal from the French king's council left the way clear for Guise, who, after being recalled from Italy (where he had advanced not much further than Rome) was appointed lieutenant-general of the kingdom. Directing his attention towards Philip's English ally (Mary Tudor had declared war on France in June), he led a surprise attack on Calais in midwinter, capturing it in only eight days. His victory turned him overnight into a national and popular hero. But mutual bankruptcy and fear of the rising tide of heresy compelled the belligerents to come to terms.

In April 1559 two peace treaties were signed at Cateau-Cambrésis: the first, between England and France, allowed France to retain Calais for eight years and then either to restore it or pay compensation for its retention. The second, and more important, treaty was between France and Spain. Apart from an exchange of towns along France's northern border (where France kept the imperial cities of Metz, Toul and Verdun), the treaty was mainly concerned with Italy where France lost everything except a few fortresses in Piedmont. The duchy of Savoy was restored to Emmanuel-Philibert, who was to marry Henry II's sister, Marguerite. Siena was left in the hands of the duke of Florence, Cosimo de' Medici. Corsica, which had been under French occupation since 1553, was returned to Genoa. Finally, the treaty provided for the marriage of Philip II with Henry II's daughter, Elizabeth of Valois [*Doc. 21*].

The peace of Cateau-Cambrésis brought to an end the long series of Italian and Habsburg–Valois wars which had torn Christendom apart for so much of the sixteenth century. It put paid to France's Italian designs for the benefit of Spain and her allies and may be taken to mark the beginning of Spain's political hegemony in Europe which lasted till the early seventeenth century. But that ascendancy probably owed more to the treaty's accidental result than to its terms, for it was in a tournament held in Paris on 30 June to celebrate the peace that Henry II was fatally wounded. At his death, ten days later, he left a widow, Catherine de' Medici, and four sickly sons of whom the eldest was only fifteen, young enough to be king but not to impose his authority. France was consequently plunged into political chaos and religious strife leading to the outbreak, three years later, of the first of her Wars of Religion.

5 THE SINEWS OF WAR

Francis I was extravagant by nature: he liked beautiful clothes and fine buildings, was generous to his relatives and friends, and revelled in costly sports and entertainments. A Venetian envoy, writing in 1546, estimated the annual cost of the court at 1.5 million *écus**. But the heaviest item of expenditure was the king's foreign policy and military campaigns. The first Italian campaign may have cost as much as 7.5 million *livres*. Even after winning the battle of Marignano, Francis promised 100,000 gold *écus* to Massimiliano Sforza as compensation for his duchy of Milan. In August 1516 Charles of Habsburg agreed to pay 100,000 gold *écus* per annum to Francis as tribute for the kingdom of Naples. This encouraged the king to be even more reckless with his money, as did the pope's permission to levy a clerical tenth. In November 1516 Francis promised large sums to the Swiss cantons and a month later agreed to pay another substantial amount to the emperor Maximilian. By June 1517 Francis had accumulated a debt roughly equal to his regular annual income, yet in 1518 he paid Henry VIII 600,000 gold *écus* for the return of Tournai. The imperial election (1519) cost him 400,000 *écus* and the Field of Cloth of Gold (1520) at least 200,000 *livres*.

A serious problem facing the king of France was how to meet the sudden and largely unpredictable costs of war; but he seems to have become aware of this problem only gradually. Francis embarked on his first war with the emperor in 1521 without having anticipated its probable cost. His initial aim was almost certainly to divert Charles V from Italy by creating troubles for him elsewhere. The strategy, however, misfired: Charles V hit back hard and Francis became involved in a protracted conflict entailing an expenditure that could not be met out of his regular income.

The most important item of military expenditure was the hiring of foreign mercenaries. Standing armies were unknown in western Europe except in a very limited sense. The French army comprised a permanent core of men-at-arms (*gens d'armes*), organised in companies under captains [47]. They were heavily armoured cavalry drawn exclusively from the nobility; but cavalry alone could no longer win wars. The victories scored by the Swiss pikemen over the Burgundian knights in the late fifteenth century had firmly established the indispensability of infantry. During the Italian Wars large numbers of foot soldiers were raised by both sides. Thus on the eve of the battle of Pavia the French army comprised about 24,000 infantry, 1,200 men-at-arms and more than 1,500 light cavalry. But no European state in the early modern period could afford to maintain such a force on a permanent footing. Infantry was raised for a specific campaign, then disbanded. Some of them were native volunteers (*aventuriers**), but the best-trained and most experienced were invariably foreign mercenaries. The most highly valued were the Swiss whose tactics were, to begin with, as effective as they were simple: they would advance against an enemy in an echelon of three compact squares, each containing 7,000 or 8,000 pikemen. If the first square failed to break through the enemy's formation, then the second or third would probably succeed. This was the nearest equivalent to tank warfare that the period had to offer. The main professional rivals of the Swiss were the German *landsknechts,** who used virtually the same tactics. If they fought on opposing sides, they gave each other no quarter.

Foreign mercenaries sold their services to the highest bidder and they did not hesitate to use blackmail in order to secure better terms. Since the cause for which they were fighting was not their own, they could be unreliable; yet, despite having defeated them at Marignano, Francis was keen to employ them. In November 1516 under the peace of Fribourg, he was allowed to hire Swiss mercenaries in exchange for a huge war indemnity and an annual subsidy to each canton in the Swiss federation. Montmorency, who was sent in 1521 to hire troops for his master in Switzerland, complained bitterly of Swiss greed: 'these people', he wrote, 'ask for so much money and are so unreasonable that it is almost impossible to satisfy them' [50, I *p.* 22]. Their lack of commitment to any higher purpose than their own enrichment was amply demonstrated in 1522 when they threatened to go home unless Marshal Lautrec, who commanded the French army in north Italy, fought a battle at once. The result was a resounding French defeat (at La Bicocca) and a humiliation for the Swiss [*Doc. 5*]. But in the absence of an adequate supply of well-trained native troops, the king of France could not dispense with the Swiss. He was also afraid that if he did not use them, the emperor would.

The cost of employing foreign mercenaries was such that in 1534 Francis tried to lessen his dependence on them by setting up seven legions of foot-soldiers recruited from within his kingdom [13, VII p. 666]. Under an ordinance* of 24 July, five provinces (Normandy, Brittany, Picardy, Languedoc and Guyenne) were to raise one legion each. The sixth was to be provided by Burgundy, Champagne and Nivernais, and the seventh by Dauphiné, Provence, Lyonnais and Auvergne. Each legion was divided into six *bandes* of a thousand men each under a captain, who was a nobleman chosen by the king (this marked a significant social upgrading of the infantry). One of the six captains was also a colonel in charge of the whole legion. The ordinance laid down a   strict code of discipline (a legionary below the rank of captain, who dared to shout, was to have his tongue pierced!) and offered rewards: outstanding valour was to be rewarded by a gold ring in imitation of the ancient Romans, and a soldier who achieved this distinction was to be allowed to rise through the ranks. On becoming a lieutenant, he was to be ennobled. The ordinance was swiftly put into effect, although it was not carried out in every particular. But the legions proved a disappointment: their discipline left much to be desired and they showed up badly in action [80]. Consequently the king had to fall back on foreign mercenaries.

It seems that Francis did not substantially change either the burden or the structure of taxation during his reign. His income from taxes rose by an annual average of 1.44 per cent, which is moderate by comparison with the average annual rise of 2.38 per cent under Louis XII and of 5.7 per cent under Henry II [67]. The *taille* rose most in absolute terms: from about 2.4 million in 1515 to some 4.6 million in 1544–45 with a fall to 3.6 million in 1547. The rate of the *gabelle* in north and central France trebled, but over the whole kingdom its value was only about 700,000 *livres* in 1547, as compared with less than 400,000 early in the reign. Other indirect taxes allegedly rose from about 1.2 million to 2.15 million. Revenues from the royal demesne, however, did not rise at all. The only tax created by Francis was levied on walled towns: in 1522 the more important ones were each asked to pay for 1,000 infantry and the lesser ones for 500.

Taxation estimates based on the yield that actually reached the king's coffers are misleading, for tax receipts were commonly spent where they were collected. In Dauphiné, for example, the estates raised 662,000 *livres* which never reached the king's treasury. Similarly, a sum of 700,000 *livres*, contributed by the estates of

Languedoc, is not recorded in the royal accounts. Thus the actual weight of taxation was certainly heavier than these accounts suggest.

In theory the clergy was exempt from royal taxation, but in practice its wealth was ruthlessly tapped by the Crown. In 1516, following the Concordat, Pope Leo X allowed Francis to levy a *décime** or tenth from the French clergy. In theory, papal permission was required before the king could levy a *décime*, but in practice he dispensed with this formality. Altogether 57 *décimes* were levied in the course of his reign, usually without papal authorisation, and the total yield has been estimated at not less than 18 million *livres* [67].

As taxation was slow to collect, Francis had to resort to expedients when faced with emergencies. He borrowed from bankers and private persons, imposed forced loans on towns, alienated crown lands and sold offices and titles of nobility. Unlike other sixteenth-century rulers, however, he did not devalue the currency to any significant extent.

Francis borrowed heavily from merchants and merchant-bankers. Hamon has identified 124 lenders in the course of the reign: 87 of them were Italians, who were mostly based in Lyons [67]. They normally expected repayment within one year; failure by the king to do so was likely to damage his credit-rating. His relations with the Lyons bankers deteriorated after 1521, and for some years they refused to assist him. They played no part in the elaborate transactions regarding his ransom.

Francis borrowed heavily from his own tax officials, who were invariably men of substance. If the tax yield was for some reason below expectation a tax official would often be asked to advance the king money. In return, he was given a warrant which allowed him to recoup the sum from the following year's tax receipts. On various occasions, the king seized the inheritance of one of his subjects. In 1519, for example, he seized that of Artus Gouffier, seigneur de Boisy, and in 1523 that of Ymbert de Batarnay, seigneur du Bouchage.

Although many towns were exempt from the *taille*, they were often asked for forced loans, which could be much heavier. Such loans were levied either on individual towns or on several towns at once. In 1515 and 1516, for example, Francis asked for sums ranging between 1,500 *livres* and 6,000 *livres* each from Toulouse, Lyons, Troyes and Angers. Paris was asked for 20,000 *livres* to help defend the kingdom against the Swiss. Sometimes a town was allowed to reimburse itself by levying a local tax (*octroi*) on some commodity, such as wine. Towns did not readily comply with the king's demands. They often pleaded poverty as an excuse. He sometimes agreed to accept less than he had asked for, but larger towns were usually more successful in obtaining concessions than smaller ones. Occasionally the king threatened to imprison recalcitrant townsmen.

An expedient much used by Francis was the alienation of crown lands by gift or sale. This was repeatedly opposed by the *Parlement* as a breach of the 'fundamental law' which proclaimed the inalienability of the royal domain [89]. However, it always ratified royal alienations, albeit under protest. In April 1517 Francis resumed all crown lands which he and his predecessors had alienated, but this was an empty gesture; soon afterwards he issued letters of exemption for past recipients of these lands.

Two fiscal expedients, which became notorious under Francis, were the sale of titles of nobility and of royal offices. The exact number of letters of ennoblement issued by the king is unknown because of a fire, which destroyed the relevant archives in 1737. As far as we know, only 183 such letters were issued, of which 153 were sold at a cost of between 100 and 300 *écus*, before 1543. As for royal offices, Francis sold them to well-to-do commoners seeking to improve their social status [94; 146], for the more important offices carried noble status with its attendant privileges, such as tax exemption. The king might give such offices as rewards for services rendered or as repayments for loans, leaving the recipients free to sell them. In addition, Francis sold *résignations* or *survivances*, which allowed office-holders to nominate their successors. The sale of offices had serious consequences in the long run as they tended to be monopolised by a limited number of families. In addition to selling existing offices, Francis also created a large number of new ones simply in order to sell them. The practice of selling public offices was a form of 'privatisation': once they had become private property, the Crown lost control of the public responsibilities attached to them. In the long run, this helped to undermine royal authority. In the seventeenth century, the Crown was forced to by-pass the office-holders, by the use of commissioners, called *intendants*.

The *trésoriers de France* and *généraux des finances* who administered the king's finances between 1515 and 1527 were closely interrelated and shared common interests. Alongside their duties to the Crown, they ran highly profitable businesses of their own. Inevitably their public and private functions overlapped, offering them speculative temptations. Given the generally chaotic state of the king's finances, it was quite easy for an official to be corrupt. An outstanding member of the financial oligarchy was Jacques de Beaune, baron of Semblançay, who played a leading part in gathering funds for Francis's first Italian campaign [114]. In January 1518, he was given powers of supervision over all the king's revenues. But it was probably as an agent of credit that he was most useful to the Crown, for he was a banker in his own right and could borrow more easily than the king, whose credit inspired less confidence.

Important as they were, the *gens de finance* did not have ultimate control of the king's fiscal policy. This lay with the king's council. One of its members, usually the Grand Master, was singled out to oversee financial business. Frequent allusions in contemporary records to Francis's elusiveness and obsession with hunting may suggest that he cared little for business. Yet, in April 1519, he spent three whole days with Semblançay and other *gens de finance*, looking for ways to raise money with which to levy troops. In 1523 he was said to be frequently at pains to advise and think about his finances. He clearly left much routine business to ministers, but did show an interest, particularly in times of crisis.

Although Francis resorted to fiscal expedients from the start of his reign, it was only in 1521, after going to war with the emperor, that the gulf between his revenues and expenses became almost unbridgeable. The cost of war between its declaration in 1521 and the king's defeat at Pavia in February 1525 was nearly 20 million *livres*. The year 1521 has been described as a 'terrible year' in terms of royal loans [67]. Within a few months the king's indebtedness to money-lenders grew at an alarming rate. By the spring of 1522 he owed one million *livres* – a level of indebtedness not repeated until the mid-1540s. On 13 September 1521 Semblançay informed Francis that he only had enough money for one month, and urged him to fight 'a good battle'. But the war dragged on, forcing the king to create and sell more offices, to sell off Crown lands, to anticipate the *taille*, and to call on the towns to pay for infantry. In 1522 the king seized church treasures worth 240,000 *livres*. Royal agents violently tore down the silver grill surrounding the shrine of St Martin at Tours in order to melt it down. At Laon cathedral, four gold statues of apostles were given similar treatment. In December the clergy were asked to contribute 1,200,000 *livres* to pay for 30,000 infantry over six months. An important innovation was the system of public credit, called *rentes sur l'Hôtel de Ville de*

Paris [109]. In September 1522 the government raised a loan of 200,000 *livres* from the Parisian public against the security of the municipal revenues. Each contributor was assured of a life annuity or *rente** carrying a rate of interest of 8⅓ per cent. The 'rentes' were, it seems, unpopular and Francis used them sparingly. The total value of *rentes* sold during his reign was 725,000 *livres*, only slightly more than one year's yield from the salt tax.

Despite all these expedients, Francis was virtually bankrupt in 1523. The budget (*état-général*) for that year estimated his income at 5,155,176 *livres* and his expenditure at 5,380,269 *livres*, leaving a deficit of 225,093 *livres*. In fact, the situation was far worse, for the officials who had drawn up the budget were extremely careless: they underestimated grossly both the receipts and expenses. The real deficit in 1523 was at least 815,269 *livres*.

By 1523, as the financial crisis deepened, Francis began to suspect his own officials of corruption. In January he set up a commission to look into their accounts. Not even Semblançay, who had done so much to help the king, was spared. In fact, he was the principal suspect, but the only fault that could be found in his accounts was a failure to distinguish clearly between the king's purse and his mother's [52]. The enquiry commission of 1523–24 was part of a more ambitious effort to improve the effectiveness of the fiscal administration. Some measure of centralisation was needed to ensure that irregular revenues were properly collected and accounted for. It was also necessary for an emergency reserve to be built up. The first step was the creation in March 1523 of a new official, called *Trésorier de l'Épargne**, with power to collect and disburse all royal revenues save those from the domain and regular taxation. Philibert Babou, who was appointed to the new post, took his oath only to the king: he was exempt from supervision by the *gens de finance* [135]. In December, the *Trésorier de l'Épargne* was empowered to receive all the king's revenues and to make payments without endorsement by the *gens de finance*, but this put too heavy a burden on his shoulders. In June 1524 he was given responsibility only for revenues from the domain and from taxation; another official, called *Receveur des parties casuelles* was given charge of the rest. Thus there were now two treasurers at the top of the fiscal pyramid, while beneath them remained a host of officials. An edict of July 1524 claimed that the new system had already proved a success, but it seems that revenues did not reach the *Épargne* as fast or as fully as had been hoped. Yet the fact that all payments were now authorised by a single official instead of a dozen meant that the king had more control over his finances. He was also better placed to know how much cash he had in hand for emergencies. Another important effect of the reforms was the loss of influence by the *trésoriers de France* and *généraux des finances*. They continued to inspect their respective districts, but ceased to share in policy-making.

In November 1526, following his return from Spain, Francis resumed his attack on corrupt financial officials. He set up a six-man commission with powers of detention and punishment equal to those of the *Parlement*. This was the effective beginning of the *Commission de la Tour Carrée*, which was officially set up as a criminal court on 17 November 1527. Its first victim was Semblançay, who was now accused of *lèse-majesté*. His trial was a travesty, his judges being government creatures or personal enemies of the accused. The verdict was never in doubt: Semblançay was found guilty and sentenced to death. On 11 August the old man (he was nearly 80) was taken to Montfaucon and hanged after waiting at the foot of the gibbet for six hours. His execution did not end the prosecution of allegedly corrupt financiers, which continued till 1536. The victims included many of Semblançay's relatives, but the only other execution was that of Jean Poncher, the treasurer for Languedoc, in September 1535. By picking on the financiers, the Crown may have been deliberately deflecting popular resentment of its exactions; the king could claim that he too was being robbed. Francis may have hoped for large financial gains from the trials, but these were to a large extent offset by the legal costs [67]. It often proved difficult for the Crown to establish the precise extent of confiscated property, and lands that had been taken over by the Crown needed to be administered. It might sell off the moveables by auction and farm out the administration of the estates, but all this took time. The process of ascertaining and recovering debts could also be long and expensive. On 23 August 1533 no less than 2 million *livres* arising out of sentences passed by the *Tour Carrée* still needed to be collected. Even so, the trials did yield significant profits to the Crown. The king accepted compositions – totalling 707,082 *livres* – from the victims. He also recovered from them offices, which he could put back on the market. No global estimate can be given of the profits accruing to him from the trials, but we can be sure that they amounted to hundreds of thousands of *livres*.

In the last two decades of Francis's reign government expenditure continued to outstrip its resources. As always, war was the biggest single drain. The war of 1536–38 may have cost 15 million *livres*.

Even peace could be costly. Diplomatic expenses rose from 10,000 *livres* in 1515 to 49,000 in 1531. The cost of the emperor's journey through France in 1539–40 was put at 200,000 *livres*. Alliances, too, had to be paid for. More than 4 million *livres* were paid to the Swiss cantons between 1516 and 1546, not counting secret bribes. In the course of his reign, Francis paid 1,784,643 *écus* to Henry VIII and 232,234 *écus* to twenty-two influential Englishmen, including Cardinal Wolsey. In 1534 Francis subsidised his allies beyond the Rhine by purchasing the county of Montbéliard from the duke of Württemberg and selling it back to him at a loss of 100,000 *écus*. A financial burden of quite exceptional weight was the ransom of 2 million *écus* imposed on Francis by the peace of Cambrai. This was paid initially as a single lump sum of 1.2 million *écus*. This was the equivalent of 4.2 tons of gold, or almost as much as the total gold imports from the New World in 1521–30. Such a prodigious outflow of gold caused severe monetary problems in France. To meet all these expenses Francis had to supplement regular taxation, which, as we have seen, did not increase hugely in his reign, by resorting to the expedients described above. By turning precious objects into cash, he helped to stimulate the circulation of money. Not even his own gold and silver plate was spared. In September 1536 he caused three cups, which he had ordered for his recent meeting with the pope, to be melted down. In February 1535 he threatened to seize the clergy's temporalities, claiming that he could not tax his lay subjects more heavily than he was already doing. The threat was not carried out, but the clergy agreed to pay three *décimes*. Between 1535 and 1537 Francis obtained the colossal sum of 3,173,000 *livres* by way of clerical tenths. Towns too were heavily mulcted. Some were forced to pay substantial sums for confirmation of their privileges. In March 1537 the king seized half of the municipal revenues for one year, and in 1541 he asked for the lot. The year 1537 was marked by a wave of forced loans. In 1538, 227 towns were asked to pay the new infantry tax. The king also continued to rely heavily on loans. About 1530 he began to repair his relations with the Italian bankers of Lyons, but he was obliged to pay high interest rates. The king was ably assisted by Cardinal Tournon, who ensured that royal debts were paid off punctually [59]. By the time war broke out in 1536, the royal finances were in much better shape than before.

Meanwhile, the reform of the fiscal administration continued. In February 1532 the ordinance of Rouen regulated the duties and functions of the *Épargne*. This laid down that its coffers would no longer follow the court, but would be fixed at the Louvre and that all the king's revenues, save the *parties casuelles**, would be paid into them. The intention behind this move was evidently to build up a reserve of ready cash. Commissioners were appointed to supervise access to the coffers, each of which had three locks and as many keys. However, the sum of 1,425,000 *livres* is known to have been disbursed on the strength of warrants assigned on local tax collectors without ever reaching the coffers at the Louvre.

The war of 1542–46 was the most costly of all Francis's wars [67]. As England joined the conflict, he was forced to spend almost two million *livres* on his navy. He also decided to protect his kingdom from imperial invasion by fortifying its north-eastern frontier. This cost another 706,000 *livres* in 1545–46. In the long term, fortresses could prove more economical than raising an army, but their garrisons had to be paid and fed. In 1547, which was a peaceful year, the upkeep of garrisons in north-east France and Piedmont cost 180,000 *livres* per month. The overall cost of the war in 1542–46 has been estimated at more than 30 million *livres*. Expenditure on such a scale necessitated a frantic search for money. The *taille* rose to 4,446,000 *livres* between 1542 and 1547, but local corruption continued to erode its yield. Indirect tax rose to 9 million *livres* in 1546. At the same time every known expedient was pushed to the limit. Between 1542 and 1546 at least twenty clerical tenths were levied by the Crown, so that the tenth became, in effect, a regular tax on the Church. The substantial contribution made by the towns between 1542 and 1546 aggravated the social crisis caused by the grain famine of 1545. In the 1540s Francis raised a huge loan on the Lyons money market. As from 1542 such loans were raised annually and renewed at each of Lyons' four fairs. The annual rate of interest was 16 per cent. By 1546 Francis owed the Lyons bankers the colossal sum of 6,860,844 *livres*. Not all the borrowed money was actually used: some of it found its way into the king's war chests at the Louvre. According to Bodin, Tournon aimed to prevent France's enemies from borrowing themselves by bringing as much foreign capital as possible into France.

Financial pressures also led Francis to continue reforming his administration. Until 1542 the royal domain was divided into four large fiscal districts, called *généralités*. In addition there were four *recettes-générales*. Now, under the edict of Cognac, the *généralités* and *recettes-générales* were sub-divided into sixteen new districts, called *recettes-générales*. Each was under a *receveur-général* who was authorised to collect all regular revenues: this eliminated the traditional distinction between the king's 'ordinary' and 'extraordinary' revenues. At the same time, the importance of the *Trésorier de l'Épargne* was enhanced. In addition to being the head of all the *receveurs-généraux*, he was responsible for locating emergency funds. Fiscal policy, however, remained firmly in the hands of the king's council: the *Trésorier* was simply its executive officer.

Francis's fiscal reforms used to be seen as the fulfilment of a master-plan in three stages, aiming at centralisation, uniformity and simplification, but recent research has suggested otherwise [121; 67]. It seems now that the king and his ministers responded to each situation as it developed and sometimes were even forced to backtrack. However, the end result of their reforms probably served the king's needs better than the system which had been handed down by King Charles VII. Though the new administration was far from perfect, important guidelines had been laid down for future reformers.

Instances of popular resistance to royal taxation under Francis I are remarkably few as compared with the early seventeenth century. His subjects had the reputation abroad of being extraordinarily docile. Thus in 1546 the Venetian ambassador wrote: 'The king has only to say I want such-and-such a sum, I order, I consent, and the thing is done as speedily as if it had been decided by the whole nation of its own volition' [15, I *p. 273*]. But royal taxation was not always accepted without protest; in 1542 it even met with open resistance in western France [63]. The occasion was Francis I's attempt to reform the salt tax. The edict of Châtellerault (June 1541) abolished the *greniers* in the *pays de grandes gabelles* and shifted the whole apparatus of state control to the area of production, which accordingly lost its privileged status. The edict also laid down severe penalties for fraud and smuggling. In April 1542 another edict reduced the level of tax but extended it to types of salt which had so far been exempt. The purpose of this legislation was clearly to increase the yield of the *gabelle* by simplifying the tax. But if this was reasonable enough, given the Crown's urgent needs, the people of the salt marshes in Guyenne thought otherwise. Seeing their livelihood threatened, they took up arms and resisted the commissioners sent out to enforce the legislation. The revolt was sufficiently serious for the king to intervene in person [*Doc. 13*].

When Francis I died several million *livres* were found in his coffers. He consequently gained the reputation of having been a brilliant businessman, who had managed to leave his son a surplus despite many years of war. The truth, alas, was rather different: in 1547 Francis owed the bankers of Lyons almost as much as his entire income for that year. It was this loan or part of it, which lay in his coffers at his death. His successor, Henry II, wisely repaid part of it within the same year, yet at the end of 1548 the debt remained 2,421,846 *livres*.

From the financial standpoint, the reign of Henry II is chiefly remembered for the *Grand Parti de Lyon*, an experiment aimed at consolidating royal loans and improving royal credit [130]. Whereas in the past the merchant bankers of Lyons had lent to the Crown as individuals and on various terms, they were now offered a new, consolidated and medium-term loan. They were promised a payment of 5 per cent quarterly at each of Lyons' four fairs. Such was the enthusiasm for the *Grand Parti* when it was first put into effect (1555) for a total of 3.4 million *livres* that the Crown was able to raise a further sum in the same way that year and also in 1556. Creditors who had lent the king money in other ways were encouraged to transfer their old claims against the city of Lyons into *Grand Parti* obligations. But in August 1557 confidence in the new loans began to waver after the French defeat at Saint-Quentin. The peace of Cateau-Cambrésis (April 1559) restored it somewhat: additional loans were incorporated into the *Grand Parti*, bringing the total of unpaid loans to about 12 million *livres*. But the accidental death of Henry II destroyed the hopes of creditors. Interest payments, which had already been reduced in 1558, stopped altogether in 1559. Although the Crown announced that they had only been suspended, the revenues of southern provinces that had been earmarked for the *Grand Parti* were directed into the royal treasury. The creditors as a group tried to put pressure on the government, but their consortium soon broke up, as each member tried to salvage something for himself from the wreckage. During the next thirty years parts of the royal obligations were paid off, but final settlement was not completed till the reign of Henry IV. Even then payment of interest was either refused or drastically curtailed [121].

6 THE CHALLENGE OF HERESY

THE PROBLEM OF DEFINITION

France was afflicted by a deep religious malaise at the end of the Middle Ages. Clerical abuses were rife, yet there is no evidence of any serious loss of faith among the people in general; new churches were built, new forms of devotion invented, pilgrimages remained as popular as ever, pious bequests were common, religious books formed the bulk of the printers' output, and art continued to dwell on sacred themes. It is likely, however, that the huge popularity of private prayer was partly due to the dissatisfaction felt by many people with the Church's teaching. The late Middle Ages witnessed a remarkable flowering of religious mysticism exemplified by the activities of the Brethren of the Common Life whose influence was carried from the Netherlands to France by John Standonck. The growth of mysticism was also a by-product of an important philosophical revolution: the triumph of nominalism* over realism* as a method of interpreting Aristotle. Christian theology, which had become deeply influenced by Aristotelian philosophy, consequently became an arid subject and its exponents, notably the doctors of the faculty of theology of the university of Paris, the Sorbonne*, mere pedantic quibblers.

The triumph of nominalism, however, did not go unchallenged. From the mid-fifteenth century humanism* began to take root in Paris. One of its earliest exponents was Guillaume Fichet, who published a number of classical and humanistic texts, but the first Frenchman to break away significantly from the scholastic tradition was Jacques Lefèvre d'Étaples. Like many of his generation, he was deeply disturbed by the state of religion. In 1472 he thought of entering a monastery, but decided that he could serve religion more effectively by remaining in the world as a teacher. He began to devote himself to the restoration of Aristotelianism by replacing the pedestrian and often misleading translations of the schoolmen (i.e. teachers in the medieval 'schools', or universities) whose programme is called scholasticism*. Lefèvre was also anxious to reform the teaching of theology. He was severely critical of the way it was being taught at the Sorbonne. It was high time, he believed, to get away from sterile discussions of the *Sentences* of Peter Lombard (*c.* 1100–60), the standard textbook of Catholic theology during the Middle Ages, and to study the neglected works of earlier writers. In 1509 he published an edition of the Psalter and, three years later, an edition of St Paul's epistles. In short, Lefèvre became an evangelical humanist, that is to say a classical scholar who aimed at instilling new life into the Christian religion by going back to the original Scriptural texts. The greatest exponent of this kind of humanism was, of course, Erasmus of Rotterdam, who visited France in the 1490s [88].

In order to achieve its purpose, evangelical humanism needed the practical assistance of influential churchmen. Generally speaking, the prelates of Renaissance France were not outstanding as spiritual leaders, but there were exceptions, notably Guillaume Briçonnet, bishop of Meaux, who, on visiting his diocese in 1518, was shocked to find his flock 'starved of divine food' and poisoned by the superstitious clap-trap of the local Franciscan friars [117]. To remedy this state of affairs, he invited Lefèvre d'Étaples to join him, along with a group of evangelical preachers who became known as the *Cercle de Meaux*. They included Gérard Roussel, Guillaume Farel, Pierre Caroli and Martial Mazurier. Inevitably their activities were bitterly resented by the Franciscans, whose livelihood depended on retaining the loyalties of the people. They accused the bishop and his collaborators of preaching heresy and turned to the Sorbonne for support.

Heresy was not unknown in France at the end of the Middle Ages, but, except in Dauphiné and Provence where there was an infiltration of Waldensianism from Piedmont (see page 69), it was not in any sense an organised movement. Erasmus described France in 1517 as 'the purest and most prosperous part of Christendom'. But this state of affairs did not last. Two years later Lutheranism first appeared in Paris. In February 1519 John Froben, the famous Basel printer, informed Luther that his works were being sold in Paris and meeting with everyone's approval. Even the Sorbonne found itself in sympathy with Luther's vigorous attack on indulgences, and this was presumably why he allowed his debate at Leipzig with John Eck to be referred to the faculty's judgement [56]. A long time elapsed, however, before the Sorbonne gave its opinion. Meanwhile, the pope threatened Luther with excommunication unless he recanted, and the reformer published the three major works which heralded his breach with Rome. These events enabled the Sorbonne to change its original terms of reference. When eventually it published its *Determinatio* (15 April 1521), condemning Luther's doctrine, it based its verdict not so much on the Leipzig articles as on his recent works, notably the *Babylonish Captivity*.

Where did Francis I stand in the matter of heresy? It is sometimes suggested that he tolerated it before 1534 and persecuted it afterwards. This view, however, fails to take into account the complex and fluid ideological situation that existed in France in the 1520s. As Lucien Febvre has written, this was a time of 'magnificent religious anarchy' when clear-cut confessions of faith still had to be worked out [57 *p. 66*]. Where, for example, was the boundary between evangelical humanism, as represented by the writings of Lefèvre d'Étaples or Erasmus, and Lutheranism? Both were strongly influenced by the revival of interest in St Paul, both were anxious to revivify Christianity through an improved understanding of Scripture, yet they were not identical. Lefèvre came to share many ideas with Luther (e.g. his belief in justification by faith alone) but he did not accept all of them (e.g. the reduced number of sacraments) and continued to hope that the Church would reform itself.

Francis had sworn an oath at his coronation to defend the Catholic faith and to extirpate heresy from the kingdom. He also bore the proud title of 'Most Christian King'. But what exactly was heresy? As far as the Sorbonne was concerned, it was quite simply any deviation from its narrow, scholastic teaching; thus it viewed evangelical humanism and Lutheranism as equally heretical. The point was clearly made by its *syndic**, Noël Béda: 'Luther's errors have entered this [kingdom] more through the works of Erasmus and Lefèvre than any others' [74, III *p. 258*]. But this was not a point of view that the king could be expected to share. He hated heresy, believing that religious toleration and national unity were incompatible, but he was not bound to accept any definition of heresy, even the Sorbonne's, if this clashed with other principles to which he was attached. Francis had long been interested in humanism and his sister, Marguerite d'Angoulême, was a close friend of Bishop Briçonnet and the *Cercle de Meaux*.

The task facing Francis, then, was that of eradicating heresy without stifling the intellectual movement which he had so far encouraged. From the first he showed himself uncompromisingly hostile to Lutheranism in its more explicit form. In June 1521 it became an offence to print or sell any religious work that had not been approved by the Sorbonne, but the *Parlement* did not find this an easy decree to enforce. On 3 August a general proclamation called on everyone in Paris possessing Lutheran works to hand them over to the *Parlement* within a week on pain of a fine and imprisonment. Yet even this measure failed to check their circulation. But if the king was ready to act against Lutheranism in the matter of book censorship, the Sorbonne wanted to use its powers against evangelical humanists as well. Sooner or later this was bound to cause trouble. In May 1523 the *Parlement* searched the home of a young aristocratic scholar, called Louis de Berquin. On his shelves were found books by himself, Luther, Melanchthon and other reformers [52, I *p. 337*]. Francis allowed the Sorbonne to examine Berquin's own writings, but the faculty tried to extend its investigation to works by Lefèvre and Erasmus. This Francis would not allow. The dean of the faculty and his colleagues were sternly rebuked by the chancellor and ordered to submit any allegedly heretical passages in Lefèvre's work to a special commission. In other words, the Sorbonne was forbidden to exercise its traditional right to judge doctrine. Rather than allow this to happen, it decided not to examine Lefèvre's work, but the *Parlement* banned its sale just the same.

Once again Francis had to intervene: he revoked the whole matter to the *Grand Conseil*, a conciliar tribunal under his direct control. He also forbade the Sorbonne to examine Berquin's works, but his letter arrived too late. Berquin's writings had already been condemned; soon afterwards he was arrested and sent to the bishop of Paris for trial on a heresy charge. On the same day, Francis revoked the suit to the *Grand Conseil* and Berquin was soon set free.

Members of the *Cercle de Meaux* also came under fire from the Sorbonne in 1523, Caroli and Mazurier being forced to recant. At the same time, the faculty condemned all editions of Scripture in French, Greek or Hebrew, a move evidently prompted by the recent publication of Lefèvre's edition of the New Testament. Once again, the king intervened: in April 1524 he forbade all discussion of Lefèvre's work, calling him a scholar highly esteemed within and outside France.

In 1525, however, Francis was taken prisoner by the emperor at the battle of Pavia. For more than a year his kingdom was administered from Lyons by his mother, Louise of Savoy, who needed the *Parlement's* help to organise the defence of northern

France against a possible English invasion. Taking advantage of her weakness, the *Parlement* submitted in April remonstrances which amounted to an indictment of royal policy over the past ten years. Though not mentioned by name, Francis was implicitly accused of protecting heretics. The regent was asked to take a firmer line. Unable to resist this pressure, she persuaded the pope to set up a special tribunal comprising two Sorbonnistes and two *parlementaires* to deal with all heresy cases independently of the ecclesiastical courts [13, IV *p. 72*]. The new judges, known as *juges-délégués**, were immediately set to work against the *Cercle de Meaux*. Despite a letter from the king ordering a suspension of the proceedings against Lefèvre, Caroli and Roussel (the king had doubtless been informed of the situation by his sister who had visited him in Spain), the *juges-délégués* were ordered by the *Parlement* to press on regardless. Thus the *Cercle de Meaux* continued to be harassed: Lefèvre, Caroli and Roussel were forced into exile. Another victim was Berquin. In 1526 he was again arrested and tried as a relapsed heretic, but his judges deferred passing sentence when they heard that the king was on his way home.

Francis's release from captivity (March 1526) brought the persecution to an end. Berquin was set free and the Meaux exiles came home: Lefèvre took charge of the royal library, Roussel became Marguerite's almoner and Caroli resumed preaching in Paris. In 1527 Francis abolished the *juges-délégués*, thereby creating the impression abroad that he was veering towards the Reformation. But this was a delusion. Francis was simply reasserting his authority after a concerted attempt by the Sorbonne and the *Parlement* to encroach upon it in his absence [*Doc. 7*]. In June 1528 he reacted strongly to the mutilation by religious dissenters of a statue of the Virgin and Child in Paris: he offered a substantial reward for information about the culprits, took part in a procession to the scene of the sacrilege and paid for a new statue of silver [*Doc. 8*]. This was the first in a series of iconoclastic outbreaks which may be taken as a sure sign that the French Reformation, at least at a popular level, was becoming more radical. For iconoclasm* was an activity less typical of Lutheranism than of the so-called Radical Reformation. An even more important difference between the two movements was the doctrine of the Eucharist. Whereas Zwingli and other Swiss reformers affirmed their Sacramentarianism* (i.e. their view of the Eucharist as a commemoration, not a sacrifice), Luther clung at least to the doctrine of the Real Presence. These differences were echoed in France where the 1520s were marked by a shift of allegiance among many reformers. Thus Farel, one of the original members of the *Cercle de Meaux*, rejected Lefèvre and Luther for Karlstadt and Zwingli. Though he worked mainly in Switzerland, he attached great importance to the conversion of his homeland and turned Neuchâtel into a base from which to launch an evangelical offensive against it. This was to have dramatic consequences, as we shall see.

Meanwhile, conflicts between Francis, on the one hand, and the *Parlement* and Sorbonne, on the other, continued. While the faculty stepped up its efforts to clean up the religious life of the court, Francis continued to protect certain evangelical scholars and preachers. His protection, however, was not foolproof: his frequent absences from Paris meant that he could be outstripped by events there, while the international situation could inhibit his freedom of action. Both factors contributed to the tragic conclusion of the Berquin affair. In March 1528 his trial was resumed before a twelve-man commission appointed by the pope at the king's request. But these judges were denounced as Lutherans by the Sorbonne, and the ever vacillating Pope Clement VII was persuaded to dismiss them. The king protested vehemently, but news that his army had been defeated in Italy forced him to back down. Berquin consequently had to face a hostile tribunal. He was found guilty and sentenced to life imprisonment. Instead of accepting this verdict, he decided to appeal to the Parlement. The king was absent at the time; the appeal was dismissed and on the same day Berquin was burned [88].

Yet even this was not a decisive triumph for the reactionaries. In 1533 Roussel was accused by the Sorbonne of preaching heresy in Marguerite's presence at the Louvre, whereupon the king set up a commission of enquiry under his chancellor. At this point the faculty backed down, but Francis was determined to impose order in Paris before he left to meet the pope in the south of France. The heresy charge against Roussel, he said, could wait until his return, but he was determined to deal at once with sedition. This meant in effect that Roussel was entrusted to the sympathetic custody of Marguerite, while his critics were banished from the capital. The king's partisanship caused a storm of indignation in university circles and provoked an attack on his sister by students of the Collège de Navarre. They put on a play in which she was shown preaching heresy at Roussel's bidding and tormenting anyone who would not listen to her. Later that month, her poem, the *Mirror of a Sinful Soul*, was included by the university in a list of suspect works [56].

On All Saints' Day 1533, Nicolas Cop, the university's new rector, delivered a sermon in the church of the Mathurins as was the custom. Its content, however, was anything but traditional since it resembled the ideas of Lefèvre, and the Sorbonne lodged a complaint with the *Parlement*. Thereupon Cop called a general meeting of the university. His sermon, he alleged, had been mis-represented and he asked that his critics be called to account. But, fearing arrest, he suddenly fled from the capital and three months later turned up in Switzerland [88]. His flight, which was closely followed by that of his young friend, John Calvin, set off a wave of repression [120]. Some fifty arrests were made and the *Parlement* and Sorbonne sent to the king, who was by then in the south of France, an alarming account of the growth of heresy in the capital. He promptly ordered the publication of two papal bulls against heresy and instructed the bishop of Paris to set up a commission to try heretics. But the persecution did not last long. As soon as Francis returned to Paris he brought it to an end, presumably because he found the situation in the capital less serious than he had been led to believe.

The religious peace lasted till the Affair of the Placards [*Doc. 11*]. Early on Sunday 18 October 1534 Parisians going to Mass were dismayed to find that during the night Protestant placards or broad-sheets attacking the doctrine of the Mass had been posted up in various public places [28; 69; 126]. It was soon reported that identical posters had been found at the same time at the château of Amboise, where the king was in residence, and in about five provincial towns. The immediate sequel was a campaign of per-secution more savage than any seen in France since the Albigensian crusade of the twelfth century. By late November six so-called Lutherans had been burned in Paris. On 9 December the king gave his blessing to the persecution in a letter to the chancellor; on 21 December he set up a special commission to try the suspects, and on 13 January 1535, shortly after his return to Paris, he banned all book printing till further notice. On 21 January Francis and all his court took part in a gigantic religious procession through the streets of the capital [6]. Afterwards he made a speech calling on all his subjects to inform on heretics, even if they were close friends or relatives. The day ended with six burnings, and many more were to suffer the same fate before the persecution ended in May. Meanwhile, additional repressive measures were taken. On 24 January seventy-three so-called Lutherans (including Caroli and the poet, Clément Marot) were ordered to give themselves up. Five days later an edict made harbourers of heretics liable to the same penalties as the heretics themselves and offered informers a quarter-share of their victims' property.

What lay behind the violent reaction to the Affair of the Placards? The answer usually given is that the king had been enraged by the discovery of a placard on the door of his bedchamber. But the evidence for this is confused [80]. Moreover, it is unlikely that a personal affront in Amboise would have produced an instant reaction far away in Paris. Intrusions on the king's privacy were not unknown [*Doc. 10*], yet they passed largely unnoticed. Nor does the king's behaviour on the morrow of the affair suggest a violent explosion of temper on his part. Was the persecution prompted by the international situation? That is even less likely, for it was a major embarrassment to the king in his negotiations with the German princes. In 1534 his agent, Guillaume du Bellay, had worked hard to heal their religious differences as a first step towards forming an anti-Habsburg coalition [32]. He was on the verge of success when the Affair of the Placards upset everything.

It cannot be assumed that the king was always directly responsible for acts done in his name. The *Parlement* could take the initiative in heresy cases which involved a disturbance of the public peace. The king would then condone or unwind what had been done in his name. In 1533, as we have seen, he had stopped the persecution on returning to Paris. Why did he not do likewise in 1535? The answer surely lies in the nature of the Protestant challenge. Whereas Cop's sermon had been an essentially moderate statement addressed to a learned audience, the placards were a violent attack on a funda-mental tenet of the Catholic faith. They exemplified the radicalism towards which French Protestantism had been moving since the 1520s. They were an affirmation of the Sacramentarian creed addressed to all the king's subjects. Indeed, we know that the placards' author was Antoine Marcourt, a French exile in Switzer-land, and that they were printed at Neuchâtel, the headquarters of Farel's evangelical offensive against France [28].

Nothing could have better suited the *Parlement* and Sorbonne than the Affair of the Placards. For years they had been repeatedly obstructed by the king in their efforts to silence the evangelical voice. Now they had him in their power: he could neither dispute the seriousness of the offence committed by the reformers nor stem the tide of popular hysteria they had provoked. Embarrassing as the persecution was to his foreign policy, it could not on this occasion be unwound. Had Francis attempted this, his credibility as the Most

Christian King would have been irreparably damaged. He therefore chose the only sensible course open to him, namely to identify himself with the persecution. The affair has been rightly regarded as a watershed in the history of the French Reformation, though usually for the wrong reason. It did not mark a change in royal policy from toleration to persecution. Francis had always opposed heresy in theory, but in the 1520s this had not been easy to define. The placards changed everything. They showed that a line did exist between orthodoxy and dissent. The 'long period of magnificent religious anarchy' may not have ended overnight, but French Protestantism had been made to look like a 'religion for rebels' [57 p. 66]. As such it had to be stamped out. Henceforth, king, *Parlement* and Sorbonne united in a common struggle against a national threat recognisable by all [65].

THE GROWTH OF PERSECUTION.

The appearance of an outspoken and militant Sacramentarianism within the French dissenting community helped to polarise opinion. Calvinism only began to make its mark in 1541 and did not become dominant in France till about 1550. Meanwhile, the term 'Lutheran' covered a wide range of unorthodox views, ranging from evangelical mysticism at one end to militant Sacramentarianism at the other. Yet the battle lines were clearer after October 1534: some people were sufficiently committed to Protestantism in one form or another to risk imprisonment, exile or death, while other less courageous spirits preferred to conform to the official faith.

Francis's attitude to heresy definitely hardened after 1534, though he continued to befriend Protestants abroad. The cruel aftermath of the Affair of the Placards gravely damaged his reputation in Germany. Imperial agents, anxious to discredit him, pointed to the shameful contrast between his treatment of his Protestant subjects and his friendly reception of envoys from the Infidel. In a famous manifesto to the Imperial Estates (1 February 1535) Francis claimed that the persecution in France had been political, not religious; he had merely punished sedition, as the estates would have done in his place. But words alone could not counter the effects of imperial propaganda; deeds were also needed. In July 1535, therefore, Francis issued the edict of Coucy, often mistakenly regarded as an act of toleration [115]. True, it ended the persecution on the ground that heresy in France had been eradicated. It also ordered the release of religious prisoners, allowed religious exiles to come home and extended a pardon to both categories. But Sacramentarians were excluded from its pardon; and those who were eligible had to abjure their faith within six months; if they relapsed, they were to be hanged [*Doc. 12*].

Limited as it was, the edict of Coucy nevertheless encouraged reformers to hope that Francis remained open to persuasion. Their hope was eloquently expressed by John Calvin in the preface to his *Institutes of the Christian Religion*, which he addressed to the king. The French evangelicals, Calvin argued, had been unfairly charged with sedition; it was the king's duty to listen to their defence [120]. It is not known whether Francis ever read this epistle, but in May 1536 he extended the pardon of Coucy to all heretics, including Sacramentarians. But the condition attached to it – abjuration within six months – remained. What is more, in spite of promises made by the king to the Swiss Protestants, persecution of their French co-religionists continued.

In June 1538 the truce of Nice ended the war between Francis and Charles V, and in July they met at Aigues-Mortes. This event was followed by a genuine attempt to heal their differences, culminating in the emperor's visit to France in the winter of 1539–40. Inevitably, this *volte-face* in French foreign policy reduced Francis's need for Protestant support in Germany and Switzerland. Within France the main result was to isolate Protestants from their friends abroad. By 1538 it had become clear to the French government that the *parlements* needed more powers to check heresy. On 1 June 1540 they were given overall control of heresy jurisdiction by the edict of Fontainebleau. Royal judges were empowered to seek out all persons, both lay and ecclesiastical, except clergy in major orders. Suspects were to be judged regardless of any privilege or franchise. All royal subjects were instructed, on pain of *lèse-majesté*, to assist in the extirpation of heresy. In August 1542, however, Francis admitted that, in spite of these measures, heresy was still making headway: he urged the ecclesiastical authorities to collaborate with the *parlements* in suppressing it. In July 1543 they were allowed to share the power of search and arrest. Thereafter decrees against heresy were issued almost uninterruptedly till the end of the reign [115].

The Sorbonne, meanwhile, provided the persecutors with doctrinal guidelines: it drew up a list of 25 articles in which Catholic dogma, worship and organisation were reaffirmed. These articles received the king's endorsement in July 1543 and were published throughout the kingdom; anyone found preaching another doctrine was to be prosecuted. Books, too, came under fire. In July 1542 Parisians were ordered to surrender all books banned by the *Parlement*, including Calvin's *Institutes*. This was followed by measures aimed at clandestine presses and for the control of the book trade. Also in 1543 the Sorbonne published the first Index of Forbidden Books, comprising 65 titles. In spite of a protest from booksellers, the Index was enlarged in 1545 and 1546. In January 1544 Calvin's *Institutes* was one of several books burnt outside Notre-Dame.

During the 1530s and 1540s heresy made deep inroads into French society [74, IV]. Among the clergy, only bishops and cathedral chapters were largely untouched; the Reformation found much support among the regular clergy, especially the mendicant friars, and the lower ranks of the secular clergy. Among the laity, the peasantry was generally unaffected, but heresy was rife in the towns, among the bourgeoisie and proletariat. The last seven years of Francis's reign saw a steep rise in the number of heresy prosecutions by the *Parlement*. Parisians had to watch a new round of public burnings, notably that of Étienne Dolet, the scholar-printer of Lyons. Outside Paris, 60 people were arrested at Meaux in September 1546. Of these, 14 were tortured and burned, four banished and the rest given various penalties; only four were released [70]. The *Parlement's* commissioners were also very active in the Loire valley and along the Atlantic coast. Elsewhere in France the action of the *parlements* was uneven. In Dauphiné, Normandy and Guyenne they were lethargic, but in the south, where Roman law held sway, they were savage. At least eighteen death sentences were passed in Toulouse between 1540 and 1549. At Aix more than sixty people were punished in fifteen months.

The most horrifying act of repression took place in Provence in 1545. This was the massacre of the Vaudois (Waldensians), a religious sect whose origins went back to the twelfth century [18; 118]. It consisted mainly of peasants living in scattered villages along the Durance valley. As early as 1526 they began to show an interest in the Reformation and, in September 1532, they adopted a new confession of faith including predestination. The Vaudois had been persecuted from an early date. In 1487 a papal crusade had been launched against them but this had been stopped by Louis XII. Under Francis, however, the persecution was resumed. In November 1540 the *parlement* of Aix issued a decree threatening to destroy the village of Mérindol whose inhabitants had failed to answer a summons. The decree was not immediately enforced, however. The king offered the Vaudois a conditional pardon, but they refused to abjure their faith. In January 1545, after the king had received alarming reports of their activities, the decree was put into effect. Troops under the command of the Baron d'Oppède sacked Mérindol, Cabrières and several other villages. Contemporary estimates of the number of victims vary widely: according to the emperor, between 6,000 and 8,000 were killed, including 700 women. Francis congratulated d'Oppède for his zeal and allowed him to accept a papal knighthood.

Under Henry II the religious crisis in France gathered pace at an alarming rate [104, II]. On the one hand, the government, now in the hands of ministers well known for their hostility to the Reformation (e.g. Montmorency, Tournon), intensified the persecution started under the previous reign; on the other hand, the various French Protestant churches, which had previously lacked a unified confession of faith and organisation, now acquired both under the powerful influence of Calvin and of pastors trained in and sent out from Geneva.

The tone of the new reign was set by the cardinal of Lorraine, who urged Henry at his coronation to act in such a way that posterity would regard him as the saviour of the Catholic Church. Such prompting was hardly necessary. Henry was coldly authoritarian and, outwardly at least, devout. During the first three years of his reign more than 500 heretics were sentenced by the *Chambre ardente*, a special court set up within the *Parlement* of Paris in October 1547 specifically to deal with heresy [*Doc. 19*]. But clerical opposition to the secular monopoly of heresy jurisdiction caused the king to introduce a change in November 1549: the right to try heresy cases was transferred to the ecclesiastical courts, except where sedition was involved. These arrangements were confirmed by the edict of Châteaubriand (27 June 1551) which, in 46 articles, sought to co-ordinate all measures taken in defence of the faith [7, XIII p. 189]. Six years later Henry thought of introducing the papal Inquisition into France, but the idea was soon dropped because of anticipated resistance from the strongly Gallican* sovereign courts*. Instead, three French cardinals were given inquisitorial powers, but they proved ineffectual. Finally, in July 1557, Henry decided to stiffen the heresy laws: under the edict of Compiègne judges were no longer allowed to vary or moderate punishments; the death penalty was to be uniformly applied to all heretics [7, XIII p. 494].

In spite of all this legislation and its vigorous application by the courts, Protestantism continued to make headway in France. Henry admitted as much in the preamble to the edict of Châteaubriand: the plague of heresy he said, had spread to many towns and all social groups. Calvinist propaganda, notably the *Histoire ecclésiastique* attributed to Théodore de Bèze [3], has created the illusion that no organised Protestant churches existed in France before 1555. This is not so, but such churches were largely left to themselves. It was to Strassburg, not Geneva, that they turned for spiritual guidance and help. Under Henry II, however, they began to take advice from Calvin, who conducted an active correspondence with them. He advised them to abstain from the sacraments until they had organised themselves on the model of his own church in Geneva. It was, in fact, the need to baptise an infant which prompted the establishment in Paris in 1555 of the first Calvinist church in France with an elected pastor and consistory. Its example was soon followed elsewhere in the kingdom. Between 1555 and 1562 eighty-eight pastors were sent from Geneva to take charge of various French churches. But their efforts to impose a Genevan discipline on them met with some resistance. It soon became clear that some form of national organisation was required to maintain cohesion among the churches – hence the pastoral synod of Poitiers held in 1557 at which a set of 'political articles' was adopted for all the churches.

Another significant development of Henry II's reign was the conversion of many high-ranking nobles to Protestantism. They included Antoine de Bourbon, head of the house of Vendôme and future king of Navarre, his brother Louis de Condé, and Montmorency's three nephews, François d'Andelot, colonel-general of the infantry, Gaspard de Coligny, admiral of France, and Cardinal Odet de Châtillon. A large number of lesser nobles, many of whom had rubbed shoulders with foreign Protestants in the recent wars, also adopted the new faith, introducing an armed element into Protestant preachings. It was also under Henry II that Protestant meetings, which had previously been clandestine, came out in the open, sometimes with disastrous consequences. Two incidents are especially noteworthy. On the night of 4 September 1557 a crowd of Parisians besieged a house in the rue Saint-Jacques where 400 Protestants had gathered. A fight ensued during which most of the Protestants managed to escape, but 130, mostly women, fell into the hands of the authorities. Of these, six noblewomen, including the dame de Graveron, were put to death by the king [Doc. 20].

The affair of the rue Saint-Jacques had the effect of making the Huguenots, as the French Protestants were now coming to be called, more brazen in their attitude to the government. They now felt that confrontation was feasible provided they had sufficient numbers and arms. Thus, for four consecutive days in May 1558, 4,000 of them, led by the king of Navarre, paraded and sang psalms each evening in the Pré-aux-Clercs, an open space within sight of the royal palaces of the Louvre and Tuileries. Equally provocative to the authorities was the meeting of Protestants which took place in Paris in May 1559. This meeting is often, but wrongly, regarded as the first national synod of the Huguenot Church. In fact, it consisted of an aristocratic pressure group whose aim was to present the king with a distinctively French confession of faith. Calvin was at first opposed to the meeting and it was only as an afterthought that he sent the confession that was eventually adopted by the assembly, with some significant amendments. Henry II's daughter, Elizabeth, was about to marry Philip II of Spain, his great rival as the champion of the Catholic faith, and there was nothing he wanted less at this moment than an argument with the Protestant nobility. On 2 June, therefore, he signed the edict of Écouen which ordered the persecution of heretics without reference to the normal legal processes [104, II]. On 10 June he held a *lit de justice* to force his hard line on the *Parlement*, some of whose members had recently inclined to lenience. Eight councillors, including Anne du Bourg, were arrested after they had spoken in defence of religious liberty. But the king did not live to see their punishment (du Bourg was burned on 23 December), for he died on 10 July. The kingdom was thereby denied effective rule just at the moment when the Huguenots had been outlawed. Flight or rebellion was the only course left to them.

7 THE KINGS AS PATRONS

The court of France was much larger than the king's family circle: it comprised his household, the households of members of his family, and an amorphous mass of hangers-on. By the close of the fifteenth century, it had become an important political institution: whoever had the king's ear shared to some extent in his power. Nobles went to court in the hope of obtaining offices, pensions or other favours [137].

The growth of the royal household (*maison du roi*) can be traced in a series of royal ordinances dating back to the thirteenth century. By 1261 it was already divided into six departments, each with its own personnel. A distinction was drawn between services to the king's person (*bouche*) and to his entourage (*commun*). Household officials were paid in money, kind or both. Payment in kind included the right to eat at court and to receive allowances of fuel, candles and fodder.

Evidence provided by payrolls suggests that the court grew in size significantly from 1494 onwards. In 1523 the king's household comprised 540 officials distributed across several departments, each with its particular function. The main departments were the chapel, the chamber and the *hôtel*. The chapel, under the Grand Almoner, catered for the king's spiritual needs; the chamber, under the First Gentleman, was concerned with the daily routine of the royal bed-chamber; the *hôtel*, under the Grand Master, fed the court. Bread, wine, fruit and candles were supplied by three sub-departments. Two kitchens catered for the king and the courtiers respectively. The *fourrière* transported the court and its furniture. A team of quarter-masters allocated lodgings according to a strict order of precedence. The *écurie* under the *Grand Écuyer* looked after the king's horses; it also had a staff of messengers and a riding school for pages. Two departments (the *vénerie* and *fauconnerie*) organised the royal hunts.

Alongside the household there was a military establishment made up of units created in different reigns. The oldest was the Scottish guard which protected the royal person. There were three companies of archers, each one hundred strong – the *Cent-Suisses* and the *Deux-cents gentilhommes*. All these troops were mounted, except the Swiss. Law and order at court was kept by a *prévôt*, assisted by three *lieutenants* and 30 archers.

The court included many permanent or semi-permanent guests, such as princes of the blood, foreign princes, high-ranking churchmen and foreign ambassadors. Many people attended on business: they included royal councillors, secretaries and notaries. Among the hangers-on were merchants and artisans, who enjoyed exemption from guild regulations.

Overall control of the court was vested in the Grand Master who drew up the annual roll of staff, supervised appointments, kept the keys to the royal residences and ensured the king's safety. Such an important office needed to be filled by someone who enjoyed the king's complete trust. For more than thirty years it was occupied by Anne de Montmorency, who was also constable of France [50].

The king's closest companions were the Gentlemen of the chamber, who were often employed on missions which might take them away from court for long periods. One way in which monarchs demonstrated their mutual trust and friendship was to exchange gentlemen of their respective chambers. Thus Francis once invited Sir Thomas Cheney, one of the gentlemen of Henry VIII's chamber, to enter his chamber as freely as that of his own master.

Francis I's court was not only larger than its predecessors; its manners were also more polished. This change is generally ascribed to the growth of Italian influence. As the king of France became a key-figure south of the Alps, Italians looked to him for aid or protection. They flocked to his court in waves that reflected the fluctuating political fortunes of their homeland. At the same time, Frenchmen served in Italy as soldiers, administrators and diplomats. They noted that women in Italy were an essential adornment of court society and that close attention was given to patronage of literature and the arts. In the light of this experience they tried to bring greater refinement to the court of France.

The court in the sixteenth century remained peripatetic, as it had been in the Middle Ages. If it tended to stay put in the winter, when the roads were little better than quagmires, it moved about continuously in the rest of the year. For the king needed to show himself to his subjects; he also spent much of his time hunting in various forests. But the king could not ignore Paris, which had become the permanent home of the *Parlement*, the highest court of law, and of other courts which had originally been part of the *Curia regis*. Only by holding a *lit de justice* in the *Parlement* could the king finally overcome its opposition to legislation. A further consideration was that Francis needed the financial assistance of wealthy Parisians. The capital was also the traditional venue for important public ceremonies.

Whenever the king visited a major town for the first time, he was given an *entrée joyeuse* [34; 38]. Originally this had been a relatively simple affair in which the townspeople had offered him victuals and fodder; but now it was a spectacular pageant. The king was met outside the town by leading citizens, wearing colourful liveries. In return for his promise to uphold the town's privileges, they would swear obedience to him and give him money or a valuable work of art. After receiving the town's keys, the king would ride under a canopy through streets lined with tapestries. Temporary buildings, such as triumphal arches, adorned with appropriate symbols glorifying the monarch, might punctuate the processional route, and side-shows were also the rule. By 1547 the symbolism had become largely classical. Thus Francis I, instead of being acclaimed as a second David or Solomon, was now hailed as the new Caesar. Allegories inspired by medieval romances were displaced by the Roman triumph. Some of the grandest entries of the century were staged for Henry II. His device – the crescent moon – was particularly appropriate to a monarch who took his role as pastor of his people so seriously [90 *pp. 24–5*].

Moving the court was tantamount to a military operation. According to Benvenuto Cellini, as many as 18,000 horses were needed for the task [10]. In 1526, when the court visited Bordeaux, stabling for 22,500 horses and mules had to be provided. Its baggage train was enormous, containing furniture, gold and silver plate, and tapestries. Only palaces regularly frequented by the court were kept permanently furnished; the rest remained empty between royal visits. Feeding the court often presented problems, but housing it could be more difficult still. Wherever possible, the king put up in one of his own *châteaux** or at the home of a nobleman. If neither was available, an inn or abbey might serve. However, relatively few courtiers could hope to share his roof: they would cast their net more widely for billets and might be reduced to sleeping under canvas.

FRANCIS I AND HENRY II AS BUILDERS

The reign of Francis I was marked by architectural activity all over France. It was characterised by a change of function and of style. Until the mid-fifteenth century the country houses of the nobility (known as *châteaux*) had been built with a view to being defended: they had thick walls, few windows, massive angle towers, machicolations*, portcullises* and moats filled with water. However, once domestic peace had returned after the Hundred Years' War, the need for such military features disappeared. They were not abandoned overnight, but were treated more as decorations or status-symbols. Large windows appeared in the walls, the angle-towers were transformed into elegant turrets and the machicolations became cornices*. At the same time the style of building underwent a revolution, as French noblemen, fighting in the Italian Wars, became acquainted with the classical architecture of the Renaissance. Even if they did not immediately understand its rules, they adopted some of its decorative features (e.g. the classical orders*, pilasters*, pediments* and medallions), which they proceeded to apply to the façades of their own, structurally Gothic, homes. Pioneers of this movement were King Charles VIII, who employed Italian craftsmen at his *château* of Amboise, and Cardinal Georges d'Amboise, who did likewise at Gaillon.

Under Francis I these trends continued. Three *châteaux* were favourite residences of the court in the first part of the reign: Amboise, Blois and Saint-Germain-en-Laye [20]. At Blois, Francis built a wing with a façade of loggias* on one side and an external spiral staircase on the other. The inspiration behind the façade was evidently Bramante's loggias at the Vatican palace in Rome which were under construction at the time. By taking them as his model, Francis showed his concern to follow Italian fashion at its best.

Even more interesting is the *château* of Chambord, situated at the heart of a large forest near Blois, where the king liked to go hunting. The plan of the *château* is essentially medieval, consisting of a square keep flanked by four round towers from which run lower buildings with towers to the angles. But the plan of the keep is unusual in that it is divided into four parts by a Greek cross*, the arms of which lead to a double-spiral staircase in the middle. This is a completely new feature which was clearly intended to lead to the terraced roof. It may have been inspired posthumously by Leonardo da' Vinci, who came to France at the king's invitation and spent the last three years of his life at Amboise [131]. He died in May 1519, well before the construction of Chambord got under way, but he left various designs for multiple staircases in his notebooks.

In March 1528, two years after returning from his Spanish prison, Francis announced his intention of spending more time in and near Paris. Although his court remained nomadic and continued to visit various parts of France, he transferred his main building activities from the Loire valley to Paris and its region. The Louvre at this time was a decrepit medieval fortress without a courtyard. Francis created one by demolishing the keep (whose foundations have been recently uncovered by excavations). The moat was filled in and approaches to the palace improved, but it was only at the end of his reign that Francis ordered Pierre Lescot to demolish the west wing of the present *Cour carrée*. The work continued after the king's death in 1547.

Nothing survives of the little *château*, popularly called 'Madrid', which the king put up in the Bois de Boulogne, just outside Paris [39]. Work on it, which began in 1528, lasted more than twenty years. It had neither courtyard nor moat. In plan, it was a rectangular mass comprising five blocks. The central block contained a large reception room (*salle*), flanked by open loggias. At the end of the building were large square pavilions containing four lodgings per floor, which were reached by spiral staircases. Altogether there were thirty-two identical lodgings, which suggests that the king liked to be on an equal footing with the select band of courtiers, who went hunting with him. The elevation of Madrid comprised two horizontal bands of open loggias running round the entire building. High-pitched roofs covered the various blocks and towers. But the most unusual feature was the decoration of brightly coloured glazed terra-cotta for which Girolamo della Robbia, a member of a famous family of Florentine ceramists, was evidently responsible. Ingenious explanations have been offered to explain the popular name given to this *château*, but a firm link has now been established with the Casa de Campo, a country house which once existed outside Madrid and which Francis may have seen during his captivity.

At Saint-Germain-en-Laye, a Parisian master-mason, called Pierre Chambiges, began rebuilding the *château* in 1539. Keeping as much of the medieval building as possible, he added two storeys and completely renovated the inner façades. His principal innovation was the terraced roof, constructed of large, superimposed stone slabs. These proved so heavy that the supporting edifice had to be strengthened with large buttresses and held together by iron tie-bars.

Although not particularly interesting architecturally, Saint-Germain was one of Francis's favourite residences. In the nearby forest, he built an ancillary residence, called La Muette, at a spot where he liked to watch the deer 'retire exhausted from the labours of the chase'. A set of building accounts for Saint-Germain covering the period from 1 January 1547 until 30 September 1550 shows how space was allocated within the *château* [128]. There were fifty-five lodgings within it and twenty-five in outbuildings. The royal apartments were on the second floor, no one, except a member of the royal family, being allowed to reside above the king. His lodging, which comprised a reception room, a chamber, wardrobe and *cabinet*, was reached by means of a staircase leading directly from the *château*'s courtyard. The king's chamber was deliberately located far from the chapel so as to give as many people as possible the chance to see him as he went to Mass each morning. Rooms at Saint-Germain were allocated according to strict rules of precedence. Ladies, married princes, and most cardinals were accommodated within the *château*, while single nobles, royal secretaries and household officials were relegated to outbuildings.

The most important *château* built by Francis was Fontainebleau. A castle, oval in shape with a gatehouse, keep and flanking towers, had existed there since the twelfth century. Francis enlarged it by building on the site of a nearby monastery, which he bought in 1529. The old and new buildings were linked by a gallery. Much of Francis's building at Fontainebleau has been destroyed. Only the north wing of the *Cour du cheval blanc* is more or less intact. The west wing was destroyed by Napoleon and the south wing was rebuilt by Louis XV who swept away the *Galerie d'Ulysse*, the longest gallery in France [25]. To-day the most important survival of Renaissance Fontainebleau is the *Galerie François Ier*, which occupies the first floor of the wing added by Lescot to the medieval keep. The royal baths were underneath and the king's library above. It was in the *Galerie François Ier* (now twice its original width and only lit from one side) that the Florentine artist, Rosso, evolved a distinctive style of interior decoration. This consists of a combination of stucco and painting. Each bay between the windows has a painted panel in the middle flanked by stucco* decorations representing nudes, herms*, *putti*, garlands of fruit and strapwork*. The meaning of these decorations has been the subject of much speculation by art historians. What is certain is that the frescoes were intended to glorify Francis's reign [36].

Rosso was followed to Fontainebleau in March 1532 by

Francesco Primaticcio, a pupil of Giulio Romano, who came recommended by the duke of Mantua. His originality may have been first manifested in the stuccoes, a technique which he had already practised in Mantua. In 1540 he was sent to Rome to collect works of art for the king of France. He came into contact with ancient sculpture and also the art of Girolamo Parmigianino and, after returning to France, developed a style exemplified by nudes with long, tapering limbs, thin necks and small heads with classical profiles.

Although Henry II was less addicted to the arts than his father, he nevertheless built a great deal. In the course of his brief reign he continued rebuilding the Louvre, erected the Château-Neuf at Saint-Germain-en-Laye, added a ballroom to Fontainebleau and carried out improvements at other royal *châteaux*, including Chambord. He also took a close interest in the *château* which Diane de Poitiers was building at Anet. At the same time, his ministers and friends competed with each other to build houses fit to receive him and the court. Anne de Montmorency carried out major works at Écouen and Chantilly. At Meudon, the cardinal of Lorraine built a famous 'grotto' to house his many treasures.

Henry II employed two outstanding architects: Pierre Lescot and Philibert de l'Orme. Lescot – a well educated man, who picked up his architectural knowledge from books – was responsible for a new wing at the Louvre. Its façade is notable for its classicism, especially its correct usage of the orders. Lescot is only known to have accepted six commissions. Among his other buildings, two deserve special mention: the *Hôtel Carnavalet*, in Paris (begun in 1545) and the *Fontaine des Innocents* which stood along the traditional route for royal entries. As for de l'Orme, he was 'the first French architect to have something of the universality of the great Italians' [30 *p. 48*]. Born in Lyons, the son of a master-mason, he went to Rome about 1533 and attracted the notice of Cardinal du Bellay, who commissioned him to build the *château* of Saint-Maur-les-Fossés. The cardinal also introduced him to Diane de Poitiers who employed him at Anet. After Henry's accession he became super-intendent of royal buildings. For the king he designed the tomb of Francis I at Saint-Denis, a chapel at Villers-Cotterêts and the Château-Neuf at Saint-Germain. When Henry died, de l'Orme was dismissed, but he was re-employed later by Catherine de' Medici to build the Tuileries and to complete Saint-Maur. De l'Orme also wrote two architectural treatises. The second, called *Architecture* (1567), though indebted to Vitruvius and Alberti, is original in both plan and treatment, and reflects the author's patriotism. Thus its proposals include a banded French Order to be added to the five Greek ones. Hardly any buildings by de l'Orme survive; our knowledge of them rests mainly on contemporary engravings.

FRANCIS I AND HENRY II AS ART PATRONS

In addition to building magnificent palaces, Francis I built up a fine collection of works of art and employed a number of leading artists, many of them Italian [106]. In 1516, following his conquest of Milan, he invited Leonardo da' Vinci to France and gave him a house near Amboise. What Leonardo did in return is uncertain. He may not have painted any pictures in France, but drawings in his notebooks dating from this period show that he was interested in canal-building, town-planning and architecture. Another major artist who came to France, was Andrea del Sarto, who painted a *Charity* for the king. According to Vasari, Francis allowed Andrea to return to Florence and gave him money with which to purchase works of art for him, but, having pocketed the money, Andrea never returned.

It was not until 1531 at Fontainebleau that Italian artists were regularly employed by the king. The first to arrive was Rosso [36]. Having come under the influence of Michelangelo and Raphael in Rome, he moved to Venice about 1529 and did a drawing of *Mars and Venus* for Pietro Aretino, who presented it to Francis. The drawing which has been plausibly interpreted as an allegory on the peace of Cambrai, may have paved the way for Rosso's invitation to France. His art at Fontainebleau was widely diffused in various forms: a number of engravings were executed by Antonio Fantuzzi, Pierre Milan and René Boyvin [125]. Six of Rosso's frescoes were reproduced as tapestries, now to be seen in Vienna. From the beginning, Rosso did more than paint murals: he designed costumes for various spectacles as well as tableware, horse-trappings and a tomb. He may also have been an architect.

For portraiture Francis I turned mainly to Jean Clouet, who came from the Low Countries [92]. He has left many chalk drawings of the king, members of his family, and courtiers. When he died in 1540, he was succeeded as royal painter by his son, François, who continued the series of court portraits into the second half of the century.

Francis also employed agents to buy works of art for his collection. Some, like Guillaume du Bellay, were French diplomats;

others, like Battista della Palla or Pietro Aretino, were Italians. Della Palla was a Florentine who had visited the French court as a political exile between 1522 and 1527. When he returned in 1528 as an envoy of the new Florentine republic, he was commissioned to buy works of art for Francis. Among his purchases were a statue of *Nature* by Tribolo and one of *Hercules* by Michelangelo. This – an early work by the master – was installed as part of a fountain at Fontainebleau, only to vanish without trace about 1714 [106].

Sculpture entered the royal collection later than paintings. In 1540 Francis commissioned Primaticcio to buy or copy antique statues in Rome. The artist returned with plaster casts of many famous classical statues, mostly at the Vatican. Some were turned into bronzes by Vignola, the future architect, who set up a foundry at Fontainebleau; others were reproduced in plaster only. Among other works of art in the king's collection was an exquisite casket made by Vallerio Belli. This is adorned with engraved panels of crystal representing scenes from the life of Christ. It was given to Francis by Pope Clement VII on the occasion of Catherine de' Medici's marriage to the future Henry II in 1533. It is now in the Pitti collection in Florence.

Some of the most valuable objects in Francis I's collection were made by the Florentine goldsmith and sculptor, Benvenuto Cellini, whose lively autobiography sheds much light on the king's artistic patronage [10; 99]. Cellini visited France twice, in 1537 and 1540. The first visit disappointed him, as the king was too busy fighting the emperor to give the artist much attention. He did, however, gain the patronage of Cardinal Ippolito d'Este who paved the way for his much more rewarding second visit, which lasted five years. Francis provided Cellini with a workshop near the Louvre, which the king and his entourage would visit from time to time [*Doc. 15*].

The first work made by Cellini for the king was a silver statue of *Jupiter*. This was part of a set of twelve life-size statues of gods and goddesses, which the king wanted to serve as candelabra for his table. Only *Jupiter* was completed and presented to the king at Fontainebleau. Another of Cellini's works for the king is the famous salt-cellar, now in Vienna. Yet another is a bronze relief of the *Nymph of Fontainebleau*. This was originally intended to adorn the entrance gateway at Fontainebleau, but eventually it was given by Henry II to his mistress, Diane de Poitiers, for her *château* at Anet.

The art of decorative painting under Henry II is mainly represented by two artists: Francesco Primaticcio and Niccolò dell'Abbate. The murals painted by Primaticcio in the *Galerie d'Ulysse* at Fontainebleau were much admired by artists who visited the palace subsequently, including Rubens [25]. Unfortunately they were destroyed with the gallery in 1739. Dell'Abbate came to Fontainebleau in 1542 bringing with him a distinctive style of figure composition deriving ultimately from the Italian artist, Antonio Correggio. His landscapes also marked a new departure in France. Meanwhile portraiture continued to flourish, its main exponents being François Clouet and Corneille de Lyon. Little is known about the latter, save that he was a Dutchman. He may have been responsible for a series of portraits characterised by their smallness, naturalistic modelling and a usually green background. Sculpture under Henry II is dominated by Jean Goujon. His most famous works, produced about the middle of the century, were the *Fontaine des Innocents* and decoration at the Louvre. The reliefs of nymphs and tritons which adorn the fountain clearly show Cellini's influence, particularly in the drapery which is disposed in close parallel folds and floats as a background to the nudes. Goujon's reliefs at the Louvre have been described as 'a paean of praise to monarchical government, its pretensions, prerogatives and obligations as well as the blessings it assures' (Wittkower). Another notable sculptor was Pierre Bontemps, who contributed the *gisants* and bas-reliefs to Francis I's tomb at Saint-Denis. Henry II was very interested in the image he projected to his subjects. Royal image-making was powerfully influenced by the cult of antiquity then sweeping through the arts and literature [90]. Images of ancient heroes were regarded as a means of stimulating a desire for martial glory. Although Francis I had been identified with Julius Caesar, it was not until Henry II's reign that the essential prerequisites for a reconstruction of a Roman triumph in art and poetry were fulfilled in France. In 1548 Henry saw in Lyons a reenactment of a gladiatorial combat as last fought in ancient Rome. It excited him so much that he asked for a repeat performance. His entry, too, was a kind of Roman triumph, but it was in Rouen in 1550 that the most consistent attempt was made to stage such a ceremony [26]. The entry fell into two parts: first, a procession of triumphal cars with hundreds of followers; secondly, the king's journey through the city under triumphal arches. One of them showed Orpheus, the Muses and Hercules in the act of destroying the Hydra; another presented the golden age above Henry's device of a crescent moon. The chariots were an even more potent evocation of a Roman triumph. The first, depicting Fame, was drawn by four winged horses and decorated with battle scenes, spoils of war and representations of death; the second showed Vesta enthroned; and the third displayed Henry II holding the insignia of state and receiving the imperial crown from the goddess Fortune. Each chariot was preceded by soldiers, cavalry, musicians and standard-bearers wearing Roman armour. The musical instruments imitated the long tubular horns and trumpets of the Romans, and, as in Caesar's triumphs, elephants carried the booty. Prisoners of war walked dejectedly in their chains. Priests followed with sacrificial lambs, while Flora and her nymphs scattered flowers of welcome. Wave after wave of citizens dressed *à la romaine* marched past the king, who viewed the triumph seated on a throne in a specially constructed gallery [90].

LITERARY PATRONAGE

Although Francis I was no scholar, he was always anxious to show that he was not only a great soldier but also a notable patron of learning. Along with other princes of his day, he also took an interest in astrology and alchemy, which were believed to hold the key to the hidden forces animating the universe. Thus, when Giulio Camillo visited Paris, the king paid him 500 gold ducats towards the completion of his 'theatre of memory', a mnemonic* device. Francis was also interested in the Cabala, the esoteric tradition of Jewish mysticism. He asked Jean Thenaud for a treatise on the subject, but Thenaud's *Cabale métrifiée* (1519) expresses the author's disapproval of the king's interest. 'It is far better', he writes, 'to be ignorant than to ask or look for what cannot be known without sinning' [81 *p. 303*].

Francis enjoyed the company of intelligent, well-educated men. His entourage included several humanists, notably Guillaume Budé, Guillaume Cop, François Demoulins and Guillaume Petit. The most important was Budé, whose major works are the *Annotationes ad Pandectas* (1508) and *De Asse* (1515). The latter – a treatise on ancient coinage – reveals Budé's ardent patriotism [91].

At the start of Francis's reign the greatest need felt by humanists was for a college devoted to the study of Greek and Hebrew, languages which were excluded from the traditional university curriculum. In February 1517 the king announced his intention to found such a college, but the outbreak of war with the emperor in 1521 caused the project to be abandoned. In 1526, after the king's return from Spain, Budé reminded him of his promise to found a college, and in March 1530 the king set up four royal lectureships in Greek and Hebrew. The creation of these *lecteurs royaux*, from whom the present *Collège de France* takes its origin, marked a major step in the advancement of education in France. Students from far and wide flocked to Paris to benefit from the free and independent tuition provided by the lecturers. Such indeed was their fame and success that additional ones were soon appointed [80].

Under Charles VIII and Louis XII poetry at the French court was dominated by a group of poets, called the *rhétoriqueurs*. Much of their output was religious, but they also served as royal propagandists. In particular, they helped to propagate such legends as that of the Trojan origin of the French monarchy. Under Francis I, poetry became more varied. Classical authors, who had been neglected hitherto, became popular and new forms of poetry (e.g. the elegy, the epistle, the eclogue, the epigram, the epitaph and the *chanson*) were developed. The leading court poet was Clément Marot, who took poetry far beyond the limits set by the *rhétoriqueurs*. His Protestant leanings, however, forced him on more than one occasion to flee the court [113].

The most important literary figure of the reign was François Rabelais, the author of *Gargantua* and *Pantagruel*. He never served at court, yet the king was aware of his work and Rabelais's *Tiers Livre* continued to circulate under the king's privilege after it had been condemned by the Sorbonne. This entitles Francis to a share of the credit for a work which has been hailed as a 'watershed in literature' [110].

A notable literary achievement of the reign was the creation of a superb library [72]. In 1518, when situated at Blois, it contained 1,626 volumes, including forty-one in Greek, four in Hebrew and two in Arabic. Some of these books had been acquired by the king's predecessors; others had come from his parents. It was probably at the bidding of Budé, who became royal librarian in 1522, that Francis began to collect rare manuscripts, especially Greek ones. Among the most assiduous book collectors on his behalf were his diplomats in Italy. While Georges d'Armagnac had fourteen Greek manuscripts copied during his four years in Rome, Guillaume Pellicier employed twelve copyists continually during his Venetian embassy. Though rich in manuscripts, the king's library contained relatively few printed books. It was presumably to remedy this weakness that the ordinance of Montpellier, generally regarded as the first law of legal deposit (i.e. the law requiring a publisher to deposit one copy of every book published to a public library owned by the state), was issued in December 1537. However, it was not strictly enforced. In 1544 the library at Blois still had only 109 printed books. It was then that the king moved his library to Fontainebleau. About the same time he ordered many books to be rebound, a task that was continued lavishly by Henry II [73]. Eventually the library was moved to Paris, where it formed the nucleus of the present *Bibliothèque nationale*.

Francis wanted his books to be accessible to scholars; hence his interest in printing. Robert Estienne, who was appointed in 1539 as the King's Printer in Hebrew and Latin and in 1542 as his Printer in Greek, explained the king's intentions as follows: 'Far from grudging to anyone the records of ancient writers which he at great and truly royal cost has procured from Italy and Greece, he intends to put them at the disposal and service of all men' [17 *p. 126*]. Three special founts of Greek type – the *grecs du roi* – cut by Claude Garamond were funded by royal grants. The first work to be published with the new type was Eusebius's *Ecclesiastical History* (1544) and the most influential was an edition of the New Testament (1550) based on nine manuscripts in the royal collection [17].

The trend towards classicism, which was expressed in the visual arts during Henry II's reign, was also manifested in literature, especially poetry. It was at this time that the *Pléiade*, a group of seven poets led by Pierre de Ronsard, came into being. The *Pléiade* has been described as 'a kind of private, informed academy, the immediate precursor of the officially constituted academies of the reigns of Charles IX and Henry III and linked to them by the closest ties' [122 *p. 19*]. Ronsard added his voice to the eulogies addressed to Henry II by artists and poets. The climax of his *Hymne à Henri II de ce nom* (1555) is a comparison between the court of France and Mount Olympus [90].

PART THREE: ASSESSMENT

8 FRENCH RENAISSANCE MONARCHY: 'POPULAR' OR 'ABSOLUTE'?

Were Francis I and Henry II absolute monarchs? There are broadly two schools of thought on this question. According to Georges Pagès, they were as powerful as any other kings of France; 'it was at the beginning of the sixteenth century that the absolute monarchy triumphed' [96 *p. 3*]. But another historian, Henri Prentout, has argued that 'absolute monarchy, if one must use this label, begins only with Louis XIV'. Historians who take it back to Francis I and beyond, he thinks, fail to see how long the kings had been 'forced to respect privileges of each estate and *pays*'. For Prentout, a more suitable label for the monarchy between 1285 and 1589 would be 'contractural' [102, II *pp. 469–74*]. More recently, the American scholar, J. Russell Major, has described it as 'popular and consultative'. It stressed legitimacy, he argues, because of its 'feudal dynastic structure' and tolerated decentralisation because its power was limited. Ultimately it depended on popular support rather than military strength and actually promoted the growth of representative institutions. Under Francis, Major concludes, 'the popular, consultative nature of the monarchy continued unmodified for the first third of the period and was only mildly altered thereafter' [85 *pp. 3–20, 126–44*]. How far does an examination of the king's policies and methods support such a contention?

Leaving aside contemporary political theory (notably, Guillaume Budé's *L'Institution du prince*, which viewed monarchy as a divinely appointed institution subject to no earthly restraints save the king's own wisdom), an examination of one or two *causes célèbres* will show how far 'consultation' outside the limits of the king's council entered into royal policy-making.

The Concordat of Bologna of 1516, whereby Francis I and Pope Leo X imposed a new regime on the Gallican church, is as good an illustration as any [*Doc. 2*] The king had just won the battle of Marignano. The duchy of Milan lay in his grasp, and, following the death of Ferdinand of Aragon, he coveted the kingdom of Naples.

The papal states stood in his path, and past experience had taught him that French monarchs had only been successful in Italy with papal support. Leo, for his part, was afraid that a French advance southward would topple his Medici kinsmen in Florence. And so king and pope struck a bargain: papal authority in France, which had been severely curtailed by the Pragmatic Sanction of Bourges (1438), was restored, and in return the king was given the legal right to control appointments to major ecclesiastical benefices within certain limits. It was a bargain utterly detested by the *Parlement* of Paris, the university of Paris and the Gallican church – by all interested parties, in fact; but its registration was forced through by the crudest intimidation. The king ordered his uncle, René of Savoy, to sit in on the *Parlement's* debates. The *Parlement* protested vigorously at this gross infringement of its liberties, but had to give way after Francis had threatened to banish some of its members and to replace them by 'worthy men'. In spite of René's presence, the *Parlement* refused to register the Concordat. This provoked the king to a paroxysm of rage: there would be only one king in France, he declared, and no senate, as in Venice. He threatened to make the *Parlement* 'trot after him' like the *Grand Conseil*, which had not yet 'gone out of court'. When two *Parlementaires*, who had conveyed the *Parlement's* protest to the king at Amboise, tried to delay their departure because of serious floods in the area, they were given a stern ultimatum: unless they had gone by 6 a.m. the following day, they would be thrown into a pit and left there for six months! Eventually, after the king had threatened to set up a rival *Parlement* in Poitiers, the Concordat was duly registered, albeit with the traditional Latin tag indicating that the court had acted under duress [136].

But this was not quite all. In 1524 Francis led a second invasion of Italy only to be defeated and captured at Pavia. For more than a year France was without a king. This offered the *Parlement* a chance to turn back the clock. It presented an unusually wide-ranging set of remonstrances to the regent, Louise of Savoy. She was asked to act more vigorously against heretics, to revoke the Concordat and to suppress *évocations** and various fiscal expedients. She professed to be impressed by the *Parlement's* submission, calling it 'to the honour of God, the exaltation of the faith and very useful and necessary to the welfare of the king and the state'. She promised to meet the demands and even to persuade her son to revoke the Concordat. In fact, she did little or nothing. By appointing the chancellor, Duprat, as archbishop of Sens and abbot of St Benoît-sur-Loire against the wishes of the chapters concerned, which claimed the right of election, she upheld the spirit, if not the letter, of the Concordat. When the king returned from captivity he firmly put the *Parlement* in its place. A *lit de justice* in 1527 began with a courageous speech by the fourth president: 'we do not question your authority,' he said, 'for this would be a kind of sacrilege and we know well that you are above the laws and that no written laws or ordinances can constrain you, but what we mean to say is that you ... should not wish to do anything that lies within your power but only that which is good and just' [52, II *pp.* 252–54]. But Francis was unrepentant. That same afternoon his council drafted an edict forbidding the *Parlement* to meddle in affairs of state, to modify royal legislation or to hear lawsuits concerned with church benefices. The *Parlement* was also required to seek annual confirmation of its powers. Adding insult to injury, Francis left the *Parlement* immediately after the edict had been communicated to its members without giving them the opportunity to reply [139] [*Doc. 7*].

Major has suggested that Francis took trouble to consult his subjects over foreign policy: 'there were,' he writes, 'many interesting meetings concerned with foreign affairs and treaties' [85 *p.* 130]. What he does not say is that it was invariably the foreign power which insisted on a treaty being formally endorsed by the *Parlements*, provincial estates, towns and other bodies, so that it should be more binding. In January 1526 Francis obtained his release from captivity by signing the treaty of Madrid, in which he promised to return the duchy of Burgundy to the emperor. Having regained his freedom, however, he repudiated the treaty on the ground that he had signed it under duress. For a long time French historians imagined that the king's action had followed a meeting of the Estates-General at Cognac at which the Burgundian delegates had proudly affirmed their loyalty to the French Crown. In fact, as Henri Hauser demonstrated many years ago, no meeting of the Estates-General was ever held [134]. The decision to break the treaty was taken by the king's council on 10 May, almost a month before the provincial estates of Burgundy met at Dijon [*Doc. 6*]. On this occasion the king was represented by the local governor, Admiral Chabot. The deputies tamely endorsed the decision of the king's council in spite of the fact that Burgundian loyalty to France was far from unanimous. The treaty of Madrid was described by the estates as 'contrary to all reason and equity' and the deputies implored Francis to let them remain under 'the very noble and very fortunate Crown of France'. Exactly the same phraseology was used a few days later by the estates of Auxonne, which suggests that Chabot had probably brought the text of their reply along with him.

The fact that Francis I and Henry II never called a meeting of the Estates-General, the principal representative institution in France under the *ancien régime*, is by itself of great interest: the two kings evidently regarded the estates as useless, if not dangerous, and never found themselves in a sufficiently weak position to be obliged to call them. The only time a meeting of the Estates-General was seriously considered was in 1525, during Francis's captivity. It was discussed by the *Parlement*, but fear was expressed that the people's representatives might be tempted to take the regent's place or to control her actions too closely. The idea was therefore dropped, and the Estates-General remained in abeyance till 1560, when a combination of religious unrest and royal insolvency forced King Charles IX to call them.

In the absence of the Estates-General, the only national body remotely comparable to them, which Francis summoned, was the Assembly of Notables of 1527 [139]. This has been called a *lit de justice*, but it was different in several respects: for example, its membership was widened to include many churchmen, representatives of the provincial *Parlements* as well as *baillis* and *sénéchaux*. The assembly was thus a compromise between a *lit de justice* and the Estates-General. Its procedure, too, was tailored to circumstances. In no sense was it a representative body, for unlike the Estates-General it was not preceded by elections. The important matters submitted to the notables would normally have been dealt with by the king's council. The assembly was, in fact, a sort of enlarged royal council designed to give an appearance of national consultation. Why?

Francis in 1527 needed an exceptionally large subsidy – 2 million gold crowns (*écus*) – with which to pay the ransom of his two sons whom he had left as hostages in Spain under the treaty of Madrid. He asked the delegates for their views on the validity of this agreement and on whether or not, having broken his word to the emperor, he was bound to return to prison. Above all, he asked for a favourable response to his demand for money. But he made it abundantly plain that he was consulting the delegates simply to honour them, not because he was under any compulsion to do so. The king's speech, however tendentious, was well received; each group of delegates met separately to consider its reply. On 20 December they gave Francis all that he wanted: the treaty of Madrid was declared null and void, as was the king's oath to the emperor.

All four groups agreed to contribute the sum demanded by Francis.

Instances of popular resistance to royal taxation under Francis are remarkably few by comparison with the number later on, especially in the early seventeenth century [*Doc. 14*]. Frenchmen had the reputation abroad of being extraordinarily compliant, but this was not altogether deserved. Royal taxation was not always accepted without protest; in 1542 it even met with open resistance in western France [63]. An attempt by the king to reform the *gabelle* or salt tax was bitterly opposed by the people of the salt marshes, who felt that their livelihood was at risk. They took up arms and resisted two waves of royal commissioners. The king was forced to summon the feudal militia (*ban-et-arrière-ban*) of Poitou, but even this did not stop the rebels, who took advantage of the fact that the king's army was fighting on several fronts at once. About 10,000 rebels equipped with artillery barred the way to the salt marshes and forced the commissioners to retire. Only the king's personal intervention brought the unrest to a halt. He sat in judgement on the rebels at La Rochelle and, after giving them the fright of their lives, pardoned them [*Doc. 13*].

Much has been made of the king's magnanimity on this occasion. It certainly compared favourably with Charles V's treatment of his own rebels at Ghent (1540). But three qualifications need to be made. First, Francis's pardon was conditional on the owners of the salt marshes delivering a large quantity of salt to the royal warehouse (*grenier*) at Rouen. This enabled the king to pay off some of his creditors in kind. Secondly, Francis could not afford to be otherwise than magnanimous in the midst of another war with the emperor. To have put down the rebellion by force would have entailed a costly diversion of military effort; it would also have left behind much bitterness in an area vulnerable to English intervention. Thirdly, Francis did not give up his long-term plans for the *gabelle*. The idea of unifying the salt tax survived: two edicts in 1544 extended the system of *greniers à sel* to the whole kingdom, except Languedoc, Dauphiné, Brittany and Provence, provoking serious riots in Saintonge two years later. In 1546 the government decided to farm out the *gabelle* for ten years and the result was that by 1548 the tax had become so oppressive as to ignite a new revolt far more serious than that of 1542. This was savagely crushed by Henry II.

So far we have been considering instances of royal authoritarianism mainly at the centre of government. But what of the periphery? How far were Francis I and Henry II able to enforce their will in the localities? We need to look at two important organs of local government: the *Parlements* and the estates.

Francis and Henry claimed absolute sovereignty over all the *Parlements*: their role, the kings affirmed, was to administer justice, not to question royal decisions. But members of the *Parlements* regarded themselves not simply as supreme judges under the king, but also as defenders of provincial rights and privileges. Consequently, they opposed the creation of offices and the imposition of extraordinary taxes. Often they were more successful in opposing the Crown than was the *Parlement* of Paris because of their distance from the centre of government: this caused delays in sending out *lettres de jussion* and made the holding of *lits de justice* difficult, if not impossible. Yet the king could make life very difficult for a *Parlement* if he set his mind to it, as the *Parlement* of Rouen discovered in 1540 [58, I]. The magistrates of Rouen had an unsavoury reputation. It was said that they wore beards, dressed dissolutely, arrived in court late or suffering from hangovers, spent too much time playing tennis, cards or at dice, frequented bawdy houses, associated with people of low station, committed grave indiscretions, took bribes and allowed improper considerations to affect their conduct as judges. The first president, Marcillac, warned them that, unless they mended their ways, the king would be forced to intervene.

Having set up the *Parlement* of Rouen, Francis was all the more put out by reports of its disreputable activities. In 1539 his anger was aroused when the *Parlement* clashed with Chancellor Poyet over the important ordinance of Villers-Cotterêts: whereas in Paris this had been registered within a month, at Rouen it met with countless delays and difficulties. Even more serious was the *Parlement's* deceitful omission of sixteen unpalatable clauses from the ordinance when finally it did register it in June 1540! On 4 August Francis forbade the court to go into recess. He announced that he would soon be coming to Rouen and would have important things to say to the court. The *Parlement* accordingly remained in session. On 26 August, in an eleventh-hour attempt to ward off disaster, it hurriedly registered the whole ordinance of Villers-Cotterêts. Nine days later it sent a deputation to the king, but he did not reassure its members. 'I will go, gentlemen, to see my *Parlement*', he said: 'the worthy will be pleased and the unworthy displeased.' Next day the *Parlement* gathered, expecting a *lit-de-justice*, but it was treated instead to a reprimand from the chancellor that lasted four hours! 'The king', he declared, 'had planted a vineyard with choice plants; he had built a winepress nearby in anticipation of the harvest; but the vines had produced only wild and sour grapes.' On 10 September the king cancelled several recent decrees by the *Parlement* and closed the court down till further notice. That same day the *Parlement* surrendered its seals to the king.

However, there was too much crime in Normandy to permit a complete suspension of royal justice. The king consequently commissioned some of the Rouen magistrates – presumably the least objectionable – to continue judging criminal cases in the town, while others were to hold *Grands Jours* at Bayeux. *Grands Jours* were commissions of *parlementaires* sent out from time to time to various parts of the kingdom in order to buttress the administration of justice and to shoulder some of the *parlements'* heavy load of work. The strengths and weaknesses of the system are well-illustrated by the *Grands Jours* of Bayeux (September 1540): the magistrates were given ample powers to deal with criminal matters, including heresy, and they got through a vast amount of business in less than three months. Yet their jurisdiction made only a limited impact, as many offenders had left the area as soon as the *Grands Jours* had been announced. Many executions had to be carried out in effigy only: a lifesize dummy of the condemned man, dressed in his own clothes, would be hanged, beheaded or broken on the wheel.

The two commissions set up by Francis in September 1540 gave the *parlementaires* of Rouen a chance to redeem themselves, and in January 1541 they got their reward. The archbishop of Rouen announced the king's decision to reopen the *Parlement* because of their good work: nine councillors, however, were excluded from the reprieve and examined by royal commissioners. All except one (who was banished from the kingdom after a long imprisonment) were eventually reinstated. They were warned, however, that the king would be keeping a close watch on them. Under Henry II the *Parlement* of Rouen successfully objected to some of the powers claimed by the provincial governor, Admiral Annebault, but the government gave way only because the admiral had been out of royal favour since the death of Francis I. Equally qualified was the *Parlement's* success in getting the *présidiaux* suppressed. Within a short time the new tribunals reappeared.

At the provincial level, representative estates existed in many parts of France – the *pays d'états*. The principal ones were Normandy, Languedoc, Dauphiné, Burgundy, Provence and Brittany [86]. In most of them the three estates were represented, but they were not always chosen in the same way, nor was their role identical from one province to another. The clergy sat as landowners, not as representatives of the Church, so as to avoid binding it to decisions taken by the estates. The nobles represented not only themselves but the rural population in general. As for the third estate, it consisted of urban representatives only. The estates were not democratic: the majority of the people, both rural and urban, had no voice.

The estates depended for their existence on the king: he called them, fixed the date and place of their meeting, appointed the president and determined their agenda. His commissioners put forward his demands, negotiated with the delegates and met some of their requests. Usually, the estates assembled once a year, but they could gather more often. The frequency of meetings was determined by the Crown's fiscal needs. In theory, the voting of a subsidy was conditional – this at least was true of Languedoc before 1538: the royal commissioners were expected to attend to the humble supplications of the estates before supply was granted. But the estates expected little of the commissioners, knowing full well that the only decisions that mattered were those taken by the king's council, which invariably came several months *after* a grant had been made. In 1538 Francis refused to accept even the theory: he ordered his commissioners at the estates of Albi not to reply to their *doléances** till supply had been granted. The estates protested, then accepted a face-saving compromise [51].

It has been argued that Francis, far from being absolute, treated the estates of Normandy with consideration [102, II *p. 473*]. It is true that he instructed his commissioners to ask the estates to grant 'freely' the sum demanded by him. But what did this freedom amount to? Certainly not the freedom to refuse the *taille* or even to demand a reduction of its amount [121]. The estates could argue only over demands for supplementary taxes (*crues*), usually to no effect. In 1516 a delegate proposed that nothing should be voted except in return for the abolition of all the 'innovations' created since the start of the reign. The 'innovations', however, survived and each year the estates voted ever larger *crues*. Under Henry II the pressure of royal fiscality on the Norman estates became if anything heavier [102, II]. Although, after 1554, the estates met only once a year, this did not mean a lessening of the tax burden on the province. Whereas Francis had made several demands within a year, Henry did so once. In June 1549 the estates agreed to pay the *taillon** as an alternative to the burden of supplying the king's army with victuals. Within a few years, however, the troops were again living off the land, while the *taillon* continued to be levied.

It is a mistake to imagine that the king could not raise taxes in the *pays d'états* without the consent of the people's representatives. In Languedoc, the towns, clergy and nobility were all subjected to impositions regardless of the estates. The accounts of a single diocese in the province reveal that as much as two-fifths of the taxes raised were unknown to the estates!

Are we to conclude from all this that the estates no longer had a significant part to play in the state? This would be an over-statement. The *doléances* they submitted to the king's commissioners were not concerned exclusively with the defence of local privileges: they dealt with many administrative and economic matters about which no fundamental disagreement existed between them and the Crown. For instance, it was mutually advantageous for corruption or negligence among royal officials to be brought to the notice of the central government and duly punished. The estates might also make some useful suggestions about trade. The seriousness with which the government viewed such suggestions is attested by comments such as 'reasonable', 'granted' or 'they will have letters on this' found in the margins of the *doléances*. Yet it has to be said that in the first half of the sixteenth century the effectiveness of the estates was limited to matters of secondary importance to the Crown: where its financial interest was at stake, the estates were virtually powerless.

To sum up, historians who have attempted to characterise the monarchy of Francis I and Henry II fall into two camps: first, those who look outwards from the centre of the kingdom; secondly, those who have approached the problem from the periphery. The former have seen the monarchy as 'absolute' and the latter as 'contractual' or 'popular and consultative'. Both views deserve serious attention. French Renaissance monarchy was limited by the foundations of medieval privilege on which it was built: royal legislation was subject to registration by the *Parlements*, and in the *pays d'états* royal taxation was subject, in theory at least, to the consent of the people's representatives. The enforcement of the law depended on a willingness to obey not always evinced by the local authorities. The evidence of the *Grands Jours* of Bayeux shows that, in an area fairly close to Paris, law and order had largely broken down by 1540. However ineffective the provincial estates may have been in resisting the Crown's fiscal pressure, they none the less survived. Clearly a monarchy whose effectiveness was subject to so many practical limitations cannot be called 'absolute' in the full sense of the word. But can it be called 'contractual' if local privileges are repeatedly flouted, or 'popular and consultative' if the bulk of the population is unrepresented and consultation is usually nothing more than a sham designed to give a veneer of respectability to preordained policies?

If constitutional labels are to mean anything, they ought surely to take into account not only the realities of power but also the intentions of the ruler. Did Francis I show respect for local autonomy or did he work for administrative uniformity within his kingdom? Many of his statements, notably the angry outbursts he directed at the *parlements*, reveal an uncompromisingly authoritarian disposition, bent on centralisation. When the estates of Languedoc claimed exemption from the garrisoning of troops, he retorted: 'this kingdom is one body and one monarchy.' All his subjects, he continued, should be treated alike since he esteemed them all equally; to exempt some would mean that others would have to bear a proportionately heavier burden. On another occasion he declared: 'in times of necessity all privileges cease, and not only privileges, but common laws as well, for necessity has no law.' The estates of Languedoc certainly did not see him as a 'contractual monarch': they complained in 1522 that they were being treated 'as if they had never had nor acquired the said privileges' [51 *p. 576*]. True, Francis did sometimes bargain with them, but only over the means of raising a sum, not over the sum itself. He did not mind suppressing offices so long as he received as much money in compensation as he would have got from their sale. Sometimes he got more! In all matters other than fiscal, the king's policy was less systematic. The estates could hope for a reversal in their favour, but in the long run royal policy seriously undermined provincial autonomy.

The political philosophy of Francis I and his successor is best summed up perhaps by the words of Chancellor Poyet to the *Parlement* of Rouen in 1540: 'the king is not asking for advice as to whether or not they [his laws] are to be obeyed: once the prince has decreed them, one must proceed; no one has the right to interpret, adjust or diminish them' [58, II *p. 9*]. Can a monarchy holding such views be deemed 'contractual' or 'popular and consultative'? Absolutism in the seventeenth-century sense of the word cannot be said to have been achieved under Francis I or Henry II (for one thing they had eleven times fewer servants to rule their fifteen million subjects than Louis XIV had to impose his will on his twenty million) but the kings' actions and informal pronouncements certainly pointed that way.

Yet, if Francis I and Henry II liked to think of themselves as 'absolute monarchs' and often rode roughshod over the rights of their subjects, the monarchy itself was by no means secure. The king had to contend with a multiplicity of local interests. Apart from the provincial estates, many towns retained substantial political and financial privileges. Taxation alone, as we have seen, could not sustain the growing burden of royal expenditure, and the expedients upon which the king was forced to rely undermined his authority. Some made him dependent on financiers, while others, notably the sale of offices, served to buttress provincialism. Royal offices became the patrimony of well-to-do provincial families who used them to defend their privileged status. The nobles through their ownership of land, their domination of the peasantry, and their capacity to use force constituted a serious obstacle in the path of an extension of royal power. Their loyalty to the Crown could not be assumed; it had to be bought by means of privileges, such as tax exemption. The system of provincial governorships could be used to enforce the king's will but also to defend noble interests. The enormous powers of patronage enjoyed by the governors could be directed against the Crown [97]. Under Francis I and Henry II such limitations on monarchy were generally contained. Except for the constable of Bourbon, the nobility proved loyal and even assisted the Crown's centralising efforts. The clergy and the towns may have complained of the fiscal burdens, but their obedience never wavered. The *parlements* and estates were also broadly submissive. And this state of affairs continued till Henry II's accidental death in 1559 deprived the ship of state of a strong hand on the tiller. The Wars of Religion which followed soon afterwards revealed the structural weakness of the Valois monarchy. For almost a century its survival hung in the balance, but in the end, under Louis XIV, it emerged more 'absolute' than ever before.

PART FOUR: DOCUMENTS

The following extracts have been chosen to illustrate some of the main themes in this book. Since it is primarily intended for students lacking a good reading knowledge of French, all the extracts have been translated. Except for the first, all the translations are my own. In the interests of readability and clarity I have taken some slight liberties with the originals: occasionally superfluous words have been omitted, names substituted for pronouns and punctuation added.

Two extracts have been taken from the manuscript registers of the *Parlement* of Paris, which are kept at the *Archives nationales* in Paris. The rest are all from printed works.

Among narrative sources three illustrating aspects of the reign of Francis I deserve a brief introduction. The *Journal de Jean Barrillon* is an invaluable source for the early years of the reign. As the secretary to Antoine Duprat, chancellor of France, Barrillon had easy access to many state documents, some of which are incorporated into his diary, which runs from 1 January 1515 till 10 December 1521. A more lively, albeit less accurate, source is the *Journal d'un bourgeois de Paris*, whose author has not been identified. He was probably a Parisian and on his own admission witnessed some of the events he describes. His *Journal* is a chronicle, not a diary compiled from day to day. As a result, its chronology is at times confusing, but it offers a valuable insight into contemporary public opinion. Though basically loyal to the king, the author's critical attitude to certain royal policies (e.g. taxation) is clear. The *Cronique du Roy Françoys premier* is another anonymous chronicle. Frequent references to Sens in the text suggest that the author may have come from that town. As for the *Mémoires de Martin et Guillaume du Bellay*, they are unique among contemporary narratives in covering the entire reign of Francis. The first part was written by Guillaume, the rest by his younger brother, Martin, who revised the entire work for publication. The authors belonged to a large and distinguished family notable for its services to church and state. Guillaume served as ambassador in England and in Germany. Between 1532 and 1534 he worked strenuously to heal the religious schism in Germany, which stood in the way of a united princely opposition to the house of Habsburg. He died in 1543. His brother, Martin, who died in 1555, was essentially a soldier. The *Mémoires* were first published in 1569.

The reign of Henry II is illustrated by extracts from four narrative sources. Brantôme (1540?–1614) was a courtier and soldier, who took to writing in early middle age after being crippled. He loved gossip and needs to be read with care. Monluc (1499?–1577) was a soldier from Gascony, who rose to become a marshal of France. He won fame in 1555 by defending Siena against the imperialists. He began drafting his memoirs in the winter of 1570–71 partly for his own enjoyment and partly to answer his detractors. Théodore de Bèze (also called Theodore Beza) (1519–1605) was a Calvinist theologian from Burgundy, who settled in Geneva in 1548, became a professor and eventually succeeded Calvin as the leader of the Swiss Calvinists. His *Histoire ecclésiastique*, published in 1580, may not be his own work, but a compilation of memoirs sent to him from all parts of France. Jacques-Auguste De Thou (1553–1617) was a distinguished lawyer and historian. Although his *Historiae sui temporis*, first published in 1604–20, was placed on the Index, he was a Catholic, albeit a strongly Gallican one.

DOCUMENT 1   SEYSSEL ON THE FRENCH
                          MONARCHY, 1515

Of these bridles by which the absolute power of the king of France is regulated I deem that there are three main ones. The first is religion, the second justice, the third the polity ...

As to the first, it is certain that the people of France have always been and still are devout and religious above all other people and nations ... So it is essential that whoever is king here make known to the people by example and by present and overt demonstration that he is a zealous observant of the Christian faith and wishes to maintain and augment it to the best of his ability. If the people had another opinion of him, they would hate him and perhaps obey him but ill ... If the king lives in accordance with the Christian religion and law [at least in appearance] he can scarcely act tyrannically, and if he does so act, it is permissible for any prelate or any other man of religion who leads a good life and holds the people in esteem to remonstrate with him and censure him and for a simple preacher to reprehend him publicly to his face ...

The second bridle is justice, which beyond any doubt is in greater authority in France than in any other country of the world that we know of, especially on account of the *Parlements*, which were instituted chiefly to bridle the absolute power that the kings might want to use. From the very outset they were staffed with such great persons in such number and of such power that the kings have always been subject to them with respect to distributive justice. So one can have justice and right against kings as well as against subjects in civil matters; and in cases between private parties the royal authority cannot prejudice the right of others, but on the contrary the king's letters and rescripts are subject to the judgments of the *Parlements*, not touching obreption and subreption only, as it is with other princes according to the Roman law, but also with respect to legality and illegality.

Royal graces and remissions in criminal cases are so thoroughly debated in *Parlement* and those who obtain them put through such interrogation that few people dare do any misdeed, through hope or confidence in them. Although occasionally, on account of the too great favor of a willful king, men dare not take legal action in such a case, yet in the long run the king repents; and so finally, when this inordinate favor has ceased, they who had it, or their heirs, are more sharply punished than if they had not made use of it. So it has been and will always be in the future. This justice is the more authoritative because the officers deputed to administer it are permanent; and it is not in the power of the king to depose them except for malfeasance, of which the cognizance is reserved to the sovereign courts in the first instance with respect to their own members, and on appeal with respect to inferior courts ...

The third bridle is that of polity, that is to say, the many ordinances, made by the kings of France themselves and afterwards confirmed and approved from time to time, which tend to the conservation of the realm in general and in detail. These have been kept for such a long time that the princes never undertake to derogate from them; and if they wanted to do so, their commands would not be obeyed, especially as to their domain and royal patrimony, which they cannot alienate except in case of necessity. Such alienation must come under the cognizance of and be approved by the sovereign courts of *parlement* and by the chambers of accounts – which in these matters proceed so deliberately and with such delay and discussion that, knowing such alienations to be neither valid nor secure and realizing that they may be required to return what they take by virtue of them, few people purchase them. Moreover, although the kings can dispose according to their whim of the yield and revenue of the realm during the time that they are its administrators, all expenditures ordinary and extraordinary must go back to the chamber of accounts, which often retrenches and limits those that are ill grounded. This law is very useful to the commonwealth for the conservation of the royal domain, whose depletion forces the king in case of a crisis to fall back on extraordinary exactions which burden and aggrieve the people. In this way, too, the overgreat liberality of princes, tending toward prodigality, is restrained.

Seyssel, [16], pp. 51–7.

DOCUMENT 2   THE CONCORDAT OF BOLOGNA, 1516

We order and decree henceforth, for all future times, in place of the said Pragmatic Constitution and all and singular chapters contained in it, as follows. In future, when any cathedrals or metropolitan sees in the said kingdom ... shall fall vacant ... their chapters and canons shall not be entitled to proceed to the election or postulation of the new prelate. In the event of such a vacancy, the king of France for the time being shall within six months, counting from the day on which the vacancy occurred, present and nominate to us and our successors as bishops of Rome, or to the Holy See, a sober and knowledgeable master or graduate in theology, or a doctor or graduate of both or either laws, taught and rigorously examined at a reputable university, who must be at least twenty-seven years old and otherwise suitable. And the person so nominated by the king shall be provided by us and our successors, or by the Holy See. And should the king fail to nominate a person so qualified, neither we nor our successors, nor the Holy See, shall be obliged to invest such a person. Within three months of our rejection of an unqualified person ... the king shall be bound to nominate another candidate qualified as set out above. Failing which, considering the need to proceed swiftly in such burdensome vacancies, we and our successors, or the Holy See shall be at liberty to provide a person qualified as stated, and shall always be able to do this in the case of vacancies occurring through death at the court of Rome, without nomination by the king ...

Ordonnances des rois de France, [13], I, pp. 442–3.

DOCUMENT 3   DUPRAT'S ECONOMIC PLAN, MARCH 1517

On 15 March 1516 [i.e. 1517] there arrived in Paris several deputies sent by the good towns of this kingdom because the king had written a month earlier, on whose advice I know not, to the good towns of his kingdom asking each of them to send two persons to him in Paris on 15 March, as the said lord wanted to enrich his kingdom and to explain to the said deputies the means of achieving this and then to ask for their advice with a view to drawing up a good ordinance.

When the said deputies had arrived in Paris, the chancellor informed the king, who was in the forest of Vincennes. He sent word that he would come to the *Parlement* on 21 March, when the said deputies would be told why he had called them. And on the said 21 March,[1] in the chamber of the *Parlement*, in the presence of the king and several princes of this kingdom, the chancellor proposed as follows ...

'This kingdom and the king's other countries, territories and lordships are, thanks to God, so opulent and fertile in all human necessities that they can do without all the other kingdoms, territories, lands and lordships, yet our neighbours cannot do without us. There are several doors through which money enters this kingdom, and others through which it leaves it, of which most tend more to luxury and excess than necessity, wherefore it is necessary to shut them so that we may draw money from our neighbours while they draw nothing from us, and to root out the avarice and ambition of certain private persons, who in order to enrich themselves by their inventions, impoverish others, and to prevent foreigners entering our kingdom and settling there in order to take the wool off our backs, all of which can be easily achieved, as you will see from the articles that the king has asked me to communicate to you ...'

After the said deputies of the good towns of the kingdom had received the said chapters, they gathered several times at the town hall of Paris with the *prévôt des marchands** and *échevins** of the said city to discuss the said chapters. But they were unable to agree, for, instead of giving their advice on the said chapters, some of the said deputies had brought with them a large *cahier* full of grievances and complaints, which they said had been voiced in their towns and which they wanted to be dealt with first, while others, preferring their own private profit to the public good, refused to give any opinion on the said chapters. Whereupon ... it was decided to disband this assembly, and the chancellor told the said deputies that the chapters given to them contained matters requiring careful and mature deliberation and that they must understand this, as it was intended to turn them into a permanent law and constitution. For this reason the king had ordered that the deputies should each receive a duplicate copy of the said chapters and that they should return to their towns, where the chapters would be read out to a full assembly of the greater and saner part of the inhabitants, who would discuss and decide whether the said chapters were good or not, and thereafter send back to the king and his council their advice signed by the clerk of the town, so that the said lord might draw up a good ordinance, and that each should return home in peace, and that the king had resolved to treat them better than any of his predecessors had done, and many other good words were said to them.

By this means the said deputies returned to their towns reasonably satisfied, and some time later each town that had sent deputies sent to the king and his council its advice in a sealed package on the chapters, which had been given to those deputies. And when the said replies were received they were dropped unopened into a large leather bag and were never mentioned again. Thus did this assembly come to an end without doing anything.

Journal de Jean Barrillon, [8], I, pp. 274–304.

---

[1]The date was, in fact, 25 March.

DOCUMENT 4   THE IMPERIAL ELECTION, 1519

On 13 January 1519 the emperor Maximilian died in a town of the archduchy of Austria. The news was immediately conveyed to the king of France by the great German bank of Fugger. He also received it from the seigneur de Marigny, his ambassador with the late emperor. Whereupon he determined to do all in his power to have himself elected emperor and to provide for this as effectively and as swiftly as possible. He began by asking the legate, Santa Maria in Porticu, to write to the pope with a view to gaining his support. Then he sent ambassadors to all the imperial electors so as to retain those who had already promised him their backing, and, if possible, to win over the rest ...

In order to attend more readily to all that would be necessary to gain the empire, the king sent to the confines of Lorraine the seigneurs d'Orval, governor of Champagne, de Bonnivet, admiral of France, and Maitre Charles Guillart, president of the *Parlement*, empowering them to send any ambassadors they would deem necessary to the quest for the empire, to receive letters from the envoys already sent to the electors and to reply to them, to promise any sums they might think appropriate to the electors and other persons, and to perform many other tasks mentioned in their instructions. After leaving Paris, they came to a small town, called Coblenz, on the far side of Lorraine, standing on the Rhine ...

At this time, the king received frequent news from his ambassadors with the imperial electors, some of whom promised him their support. They included the archbishop of Trier, the marquis of Brandenburg (with whom the king agreed to sign a new treaty and to renew his promise of the hand of Madame Renée, the queen's sister, for the marquis's eldest son) and the count palatine. As for the duke of Saxony, he refused to make promises to either party. The king of Poland promised to support the king, but he had no voice in the election.

In order to raise the large amount of money needed for the imperial election, namely to pay for diplomatic missions, for large bribes to some of the electors and German princes, and for other necessary expenses, the king created several royal offices in his kingdom. Eight councillors and a president were created in each of the *Parlements* of Toulouse, Bordeaux and Rouen, as well as councillors in some of the *bailliages* and *sénéchaussées*. The king also planned to create twenty councillors in the *parlement* of Paris, but for various reasons advanced by the court, this creation did not take place. It was decided instead that the *Grands Jours* would be held in vacation time each year in the *bailliages* and *sénéchaussées*, as had been done of old. The king, moverover, raised loans from certain prelates and private persons in his kingdom; he also alienated and mortgaged part of his demesne ...

The imperial electors were under strong pressure from the king, on the one hand, and from the Catholic King [i.e. the king of Spain] on the other. While some declared themselves, the rest did not.

The seigneur d'Orval, the admiral and president Guillart, who were on the border of Lorraine and on the German marches, acted as speedily as possible and spared no effort. On the other side, the count of Nassau and the ambassadors of the Catholic King did everything possible and more. They caused to be published in Germany from the pulpits of parish churches and in sermons that if the king of France became emperor, he would try to hold the Germans in as much subjection as he did the French and would tax them at his pleasure, and other things to the king's discredit, so as to stir up the Germans against him.

After the king had been informed by the bishop of Brandenburg, president of the marquis of Brandenburg's council, that the imperial electors had been told that he [the king] was not eligible as emperor because he was neither a German nor of the German nation, legal arguments were sent secretly to the bishop proving that someone, who was not German by birth, could be elected emperor, so that he might have them published in Frankfurt, the site of the election, and throughout Germany ...

Journal de Jean Barrillon, [8], II, pp. 116–26.

DOCUMENT 5 THE SEMBLANÇAY AFFAIR, 1523

That the king should have cold-shouldered the seigneur de Lautrec on his return to France is hardly surprising; Francis blamed him for the loss of his duchy of Milan and would not speak to him. But Lautrec, wishing to justify himself, managed to approach the king and complained of his attitude towards him. The king replied that he had good reason for this, since Lautrec had lost him such an inheritance as the duchy of Milan. Lautrec replied that it was the king, not himself, who had lost it, for he had warned Francis many times that unless the king sent him money, he would not be able to control the *gendarmerie*, which had served for eighteen months without pay and to the limit, or the Swiss, who had forced him to fight at his disadvantage, which would not have happened if they had been paid. His Majesty replied that he had sent 400,000 crowns when Lautrec had asked for them, but Lautrec retorted that he had never seen this money, although he had seen the king's letter promising it. At this juncture the seigneur de Semblançay, superintendent of the finances of France, was summoned. He admitted that he had received the king's command to send the money, but explained that as it was awaiting dispatch it was seized by the king's mother, the regent, and he offered to prove this forthwith. With an angry countenance the king went to his mother's chamber and complained of the injury she had done him; by detaining money intended to rescue his army, she had brought about the loss of his duchy, which he would never have thought her capable of doing. She rebutted the charge, whereupon Semblançay was called and maintained that his story was true.

She declared that the money formed part of her savings, which had been in Semblançay's keeping for a long time, but he denied this. Commissioners were appointed to settle this quarrel, but the chancellor Duprat (who had long hated Semblançay through jealousy of his favour with the king and of the authority he wielded over the finances), seeing that Madame was indebted to Semblançay and not the reverse, turned the king's mind against Semblançay before the matter could be resolved and had judges and commissioners appointed to try him.

Mémoires de Martin et Guillaume du Bellay, [11], I, pp. 233–4.

DOCUMENT 6   THE PEACE OF MADRID REPUDIATED, MAY 1526

In May 1526 Charles de Lannoy, viceroy of Naples, visited Cognac in the hope of persuading Francis I to ratify the peace of Madrid.

The king in his council. Also present: the duke of Vendôme, the chancellor, the seigneurs de Lautrec, Montmorency, grand master and marshal of France, the *grand sénéchal* of Normandy, the grand esquire, the archbishop of Bourges, the first president of [the *Parlement* of] Paris and the seigneur d'Alluye, treasurer of France.

It has been resolved that the viceroy will be called to the council tomorrow, and after his demands have been heard, they will be answered. First, should he speak of the king's promises, oath and obligation, he will be told that the king is under no obligation whatever and that he is not bound to keep his promises, since they [the imperialists] did not trust his word, but kept him under guard, setting him free only after they had received hostages. Nor is he obliged to keep promises which may be attributed to him, since they were extorted from him under the fear of life imprisonment and of death consequent on the grave illness caused by melancholy into which he had fallen. He feared also that his mother would not be able to carry the regency for long, given the onerous nature of the task and her sorrow over the king's capture. He was afraid, too, that the kingdom would fall into ruin and civil strife and that his children, who are young, would be cheated of their inheritance.

Should the viceroy demand ratification of the treaty etc. he will be told that, for the reasons stated above, the king is not bound to ratify it, since it is null and void. However, regarding the treaty signed by his mother's ambassadors, the emperor has no need to worry about the delay that has occurred so far for reasons which have already been given to him in writing. One has to distinguish between two sorts of promises in the treaty: one depends on the king's free will and authority; the other, on the will of others. With regard to the first kind, the king has fulfilled most of his promises, and is ready to accomplish the rest provided his hostages are returned. As for the promises that depend on the will of others, he has tried to carry them out, but has run into many obstacles which will be difficult to overcome. He is not bound to ratify promises which cannot be fulfilled and it would be unreasonable of him to do so. Nor does he want to return to prison: no one has yet been able to force this promise out of him, and he is not inclined to cede now. Thus, if the king gets his hostages back or at least receives a sufficient assurance that this will happen, he will be happy to ratify the treaty and to do all that lies in his power, justly and honestly, except return to prison. He hopes that the emperor will consider these things favorably and will want to live in peace and union with him, as the king himself dearly wants, and that he will deliver his wife to him.

Paris, Archives nationales, J. 666/4 *bis*, printed in Hauser, [134], pp. 160–2.

DOCUMENT 7   **EDICT DEFINING THE *PARLEMENT'S* POWERS, JULY 1527**

... To Messieurs the presidents and councillors of his court of *Parlement* ...

The king forbids you to meddle in any way in affairs of state or in anything other than justice and commands that each year you shall obtain letters confirming your delegated authority, as was done formerly.

He forbids you to judge all matters archiepiscopal, episcopal and abbatial, and declares null and void any attempt by you to contravene this ban. He also cancels all the limitations imposed by you on the power and regency of his mother. He has revoked and annulled all that you have attempted in dealing with cases on appeal, appointments, etc.

The king confirms all that was done and commanded by the regent, and letters close will be sent to all who request them in their own interest. He tells you now, as in the past, that in the event of his leaving the kingdom, he appoints the said lady as regent and gives her such authority and power as he himself has without reservation. He orders that all that has been registered by the *Parlement* against her authority shall be sent to him for cancellation within a fortnight; the clerk of the court [*greffier*] shall see that this is done on pain of losing his office.

The king forbids the court to apply in future any limitation, modification or restriction to his ordinances, edicts and charters. Should members of the court find it necessary in the interest of the king or the state to add or remove something, they will bring this to the king's notice.

The king declares that you have no jurisdiction or power over the chancellor of France. This belongs to the king alone and no one else. Consequently, he has cancelled all your acts directed against the chancellor as being those of private persons without jurisdiction over him. He orders you to remove from and to cancel in your registers all acts against the chancellor and orders the clerk of the court, on the aforementioned pain, to bring the register to him so that he may see that these acts have been cancelled.

Each day the king receives major complaints about the maladministration of justice and the high costs incurred by legal parties. Today you have informed the king that this is due to *parlementaires* who have bought their offices and to some old and reputedly wise ones who cause justice to be administered in several places so as to avoid costs. Moreover, the king has known for some time that close family relationships among the members of the court are a cause of disorder. He will, therefore, appoint commissioners to look into all this and will provide for the good of his kingdom and the discharge of his conscience.

The king wishes the present edict to be registered by his *Conseil étroit* [or *Conseil des affaires*] *Grand Conseil*, and *Parlement*.

Given in the king's *Conseil étroit*, the following being present: the king of Navarre, the duke of Vendôme, the count of Saint-Pol, the archbishop of Sens, chancellor of France, the grand master, the grand esquire of France, the *grand sénéchal* of Normandy, the first chamberlain, the archbishop of Bourges and the seigneur d'Alluye, councillor and *chambellan ordinaire*. The 24th day of July, 1527. Signed: Robertet.

Ordonnances des rois de France, [13], V, No. 463, pp. 81–3.

DOCUMENT 8   ICONOCLASM IN PARIS, JUNE 1528

On the night of Monday 1 June 1528, the day after Whit Sunday, a remarkable event occurred in Paris. Some heretics attacked a stone statue of the Virgin and Child standing at a street corner against the house of Louis de Harlay, seigneur de Beaumont ... Striking several knife blows, they cut off her head and that of the child, our Lord, but the identity of the image-breakers was unknown. When the king, who was residing in Paris, was told of the incident, he was allegedly so angry and shocked that he wept copiously. Within two days he had a proclamation read out to the sound of trumpets at the town's thoroughfares: anyone knowing who had done this deed was to inform the legal authorities and the king; the king himself would give a reward of a thousand gold crowns for such information; finally, great care was to be taken not to withhold it. Yet, in spite of the king's efforts and those of commissioners appointed to conduct a house-to-house search, no information was forthcoming ...

On Friday 12 June general processions were held in all the parish churches of Paris and the four mendicant orders were present along with all the clergy of Notre-Dame and of the Sainte Chapelle, carrying banners, crosses and many sacred relics. They went in procession to the church of Sainte Catherine du Val des Escolliers, where the king and all the nobility had gathered. The king, after hearing Mass in the said church, joined the procession. He was bareheaded and held a candle of white wax. Accompanying him were many lords and noblemen, each holding a candle. Also present was the bishop of Lisieux, the king's Grand Almoner. Wearing his pontificals, he carried a beautiful statue in silver, which the king had commissioned. It was about 2 feet tall, like the other, and allegedly weighed 8 marks of silver. Walking in front of the king, the bishop carried the said statue to the site and placed it on the top of the wooden scaffolding that had been erected there. The king and the bishop with great humility then placed it on the pedestal where the other had been ...

Journal d'un bourgeois de Paris, [9], pp. 290–3.

DOCUMENT 9   THE *GRAND REBEINE* OF LYONS, APRIL
1529

In the year 1529 on Sunday 25 April after Easter a great riot took place in Lyons caused by the high cost of grain over a period of about three months, so that a *bichet* of grain [measure of Lyons] was worth 38 *sols*, 8 *bichets* being roughly equivalent to a *setier** [measure of Paris]. Thus, taking the Parisian measure, a *setier* at Lyons cost 15 *livres* 4 *sols*. This high price was caused by a dearth of grain; it was not reaching Lyons by the river Saône and this was blamed on the avarice of grain merchants. As a result the poor rioted and the city feared that it would be sacked. A number of houses were pillaged and ransacked, among them the house of a local doctor, called Master Symphorien Champier, who lived near the Cordeliers [i.e. the Franciscan monastery]. He suffered pillage and was nearly killed because he had rebuked the rioters. Likewise a rich pastry-cook of the city, who reprimanded them, was killed and his house along with others plundered. The governors of the city informed the king at Blois of the uprising, whereupon he sent the *prévôt de l'hôtel** with a commission to execute justice. After his preliminary enquiry about twenty of the rioters were hanged or strangled, while many others fled from the city for fear of being hanged ... That same year grain was also dear in Italy, notably in Genoa and Milan, where it cost more than 12 ducats per *setier* [measure of Paris] and in Rome more than 20 ducats. In Paris and throughout the kingdom it was also very expensive; in Paris the *setier* cost 4 to 5 *livres*.

Journal d'un bourgeois de Paris, [9], pp. 322–3.

DOCUMENT 10   LAWLESSNESS AND POVERTY IN PARIS, 1533

On 7 January 1533 the seigneur de la Mothe-au-Groing, prévôt de l'hôtel, came to the Parlement of Paris with a message from the king urging the court to speed up a lawsuit. He took the opportunity to raise the following matters:

He said that every night in this city some unknown persons gather in various troops and bands, who do nothing else than brawl during the night, and they have had the temerity to enter the king's chamber at the Louvre and that three, carrying weapons under their cloaks, had been caught, who might inform on their fellows and that it was necessary to strengthen the watch of this city so as to avoid all seditions, tumults and scandals. To this effect the king had ordered him to go this day to the town hall in order to deal with this business. The king had also commanded him to confer with the governors of the city concerning the problem of the poor, because a large number were to be found within it and even around the king's lodging in spite of the fact that the court had offered good and holy provision and that the king had instructed it to take such action as it would deem necessary regarding the said poor, notwithstanding any oppositions or appeals.

Archives nationales, X^{la} 1536, [1], f. 68v.

DOCUMENT 11   THE PLACARD OF OCTOBER 1534

True articles on the horrible, great and insufferable papal Mass devised in direct opposition to the Last Supper.

I call on heaven and earth to bear witness to the truth against this pompous and proud papal Mass by which the world (unless God soon provides a remedy) is being and will be completely destroyed, and in which our Lord is so outrageously blasphemed and the people seduced and blinded. This can no longer be tolerated, but in order that each may understand the matter more easily it is convenient to proceed by articles:

First, every faithful Christian must know that our Lord and Saviour, Jesus Christ, has given His body, soul, life and blood for our sanctification in a perfect sacrifice. This cannot be repeated by anyone who does not hold that it was ineffectual, insufficient and imperfect, an idea, which, spoken or not, is a horrible and execrable blasphemy. Yet the world is still crowded in many places with wretched sacrificers, who, setting themselves up as our redeemers, take the place of Jesus Christ or profess to be His companions ... I ask them all whether their own sacrifice is perfect or imperfect? If it is imperfect, why do they deceive the people? If it is perfect, why must it be repeated? Come forward, sacrificers, and reply, if you can!

Secondly, through this wretched Mass almost everyone is being led into public idolatry, for it is falsely claimed that Jesus Christ is bodily present in the bread and wine. Not only is this not taught by Holy Scripture and our faith; it is clean contrary to that teaching, for Jesus Christ after His resurrection went to heaven and is now sitting on the right hand of God the Father, whence He shall come to judge the living and the dead ... It follows that if His body is in heaven, He is not on earth; and if He were on earth, He would not be in heaven, for no one can be in two places at once ...

Thirdly, these wretched sacrificers, compounding their error, claim that once they have whispered or spoken over the bread and wine, these disappear, and that through Transubstantiation (such is their fondness for long and inflated words!) Jesus Christ is concealed within the accidents of the bread and wine. This is the doctrine of devils and contrary to Scripture. I ask these fat monks where they have found this fine word Transubstantiation? St Paul, St Matthew, St Mark, St Luke and the ancient fathers never speak thus: when they write of the Last Supper they refer quite simply only to bread and wine ... Who then will tolerate such charlatans, pests and false antichrists? ... As enemies of God and Holy Writ let them be rejected and utterly detested!

Fourthly, the product of the Mass is quite unlike that of the Last Supper, which is not miraculous, for Christ and Belial have nothing in common. The product of the Last Supper is to proclaim publicly one's faith and certainty in salvation and to remember the death and passion of Jesus Christ, who has redeemed us from damnation, also the great charity and love He has shown to us by sacrificing His life and purging us with His blood. As we each take bread and a drink, we are reminded that we must all live and die in Jesus Christ ... But the product of the Mass is quite otherwise: for all knowledge of Jesus Christ is wiped out, the Gospel is not preached and time is taken up with bell-ringing, howling, chanting, ceremonies, illuminations, censings, disguises and all manner of monkey-tricks whereby the people, like lambs and sheep, are led astray and devoured by these ravenous wolves ... Thanks to the Mass, they have destroyed everything and disinherited kings and princes, merchants and lords. Thanks to the Mass, they lead carefree lives: they need not work, let alone study. No wonder they defend it by killing, burning, destroying or wounding anyone who contradicts them. They have but force on their side ... The truth threatens them, the truth pursues them, the truth frightens them. Soon it will destroy them. Fiat, fiat. Amen.

Printed in Hari, [69], pp. 114–19.

DOCUMENT 12   THE EDICT OF COUCY, JULY 1535

Francis, by the grace of God etc ...

Since by the grace and mercy of God, our creator, the heresies and new sects contrary and damaging to the holy faith and catholic law of His church ... have ceased and are ceasing to exist, thanks in part to divine mercy and kindness and in part to the diligence we have applied and are applying under His authority in punishing in an exemplary manner many of the sectaries and imitators of the said errors ...

We say and declare by these presents that our will and intention is that those who are charged and accused of the said errors, as well as those who are under suspicion and not yet accused or prosecuted, should not be pursued or harassed on account of the said errors; but if they are held prisoner or their goods have been seized or confiscated, we want them to be delivered and set free and their goods to be returned to them in full.

And we allow exiles and fugitives to return to our said kingdom, countries, lands and lordships and to stay and live there in as much safety and freedom as they enjoyed hitherto, notwithstanding the banishments and confiscations of their persons and goods pronounced on account of their said contumacies.

Provided that they are bound to live as good and true Catholic Christians and desist from their said errors, which they will need to abjure canonically within the next six months, starting on the day of publication of these presents before their diocesans or their vicars and officials, and in the presence of the inquisitor of the faith or his vicar; provided also that if they return and relapse into crime they shall be punished strictly and harshly in accordance with the gravity of their offence.

And we do not intend Sacramentarians or those who have formally abjured in the past and have since lapsed to be included in these presents, but they are to be punished according to their faults. Furthermore, all are forbidden, on pain of hanging and of being held and reputed as rebels and disturbers of the public peace, to read, dogmatise, translate, compose or print, either publicly or privately, any doctrine contrary to the Christian faith.

Ordonnances des rois de France, [13], VII, No. 701, pp. 248–51.

DOCUMENT 13   THE KING'S MAGNANIMITY: LA ROCHELLE, 1543

... the king spoke and showed to the inhabitants of the Isles and of La Rochelle the offence, which they had committed against his Most Christian Majesty at a time when he, on the one hand, and his sons, on the other, were busy defending the kingdom, including the people of the said Isles and of La Rochelle. For this reason their persons and goods deserved to be seized, yet, as a prince, he could not and did not wish to refuse a pardon to those who begged for it, for a grace that is requested and long deferred is already half conceded, and also because their offence was the result of thoughtlessness rather than premeditated malice. He was not going to punish them as required in view of their repentance and admission that they had done wrong, for he did not wish to harm their persons or seize their goods, as had recently happened to the people of Ghent. All he wanted was the love of his subjects and he forgave all their offences, both civil and criminal. He said that he would forget them and advised his subjects to do likewise. He wanted the keys, artillery, weapons and sticks, which had been taken from them, to be restored to them, and placed his whole trust in them for the safe-keeping and defence of La Rochelle. He ordered the seigneur de Jarnac to remove the troops who were in the town ... And as the people of the Isles and of La Rochelle rejoiced greatly over this sentence, a great and sweet harmony was heard, sung by choristers in the belfry of St Bartholomew's church. The bells of the said church then began to ring and all the other bells in the town, which had been silent since Saturday at 4 p.m. joined in, producing a marvellous noise ...

Cronique du Roy Françoys, [6], pp. 420–1.

DOCUMENT 14   THE KING'S SEVERITY: THE SACK OF LAGNY, 1544

... for the correction and punishment of acts of disobedience and rebellions ... perpetuated by the inhabitants of Lagny in the month of September last past [i.e. 1544] the king commanded the seigneur de Lorges, knight of the order [of St Michael], to force his way into the said town and to sack it as an enemy to and rebel against his authority. Being satisfied with all that de Lorges and his captains and soldiers had accomplished in the matter, the king endorsed and approved of their actions in letters patent under his signature. He forbade the inhabitants of Lagny to undertake any legal proceedings against de Lorges, his captains and soldiers unless they wished to disobey him and incur his wrath again. He also forbade the *Parlement* and all other judges to hold any court or exercise any jurisdiction in respect of this matter, adding that if any of the said captains and soldiers had been prosecuted by them, they were to be released and no further action taken against them, silence being imposed on the *Parlement's procureur-général* and on the said inhabitants. The king moreover ordered the *Parlement* to allow de Lorges, his captains and soldiers to benefit from the ratification of the said letters patent fully, peacefully and without any sort of hindrance ...

Archives nationales, X^{la} 1556, [2], f. 84a–b.

DOCUMENT 15   A ROYAL VISIT TO BENVENUTO CELLINI'S WORKSHOP, *c.* 1544

Shortly after his arrival in France in 1540, Cellini was commissioned by Francis I to make twelve candelabra, each of which was to be a life-size silver statue of a god or goddess. Only one – the Jupiter – was actually completed and presented to the king at Fontainebleau. The following passage, describing a royal visit to Cellini's workshop at the Petit Nesle in Paris, shows the close interest taken by Francis in the artist's work.

When I returned to Paris, the great favour shown me by the King made me a mark for all men's admiration. I received the silver and began my statue of Jupiter. Many journeymen were now in my employ; and the work went onward briskly day and night; so that, by the time I had finished the clay models of Jupiter, Vulcan and Mars, and had begun to get the silver statue forward, my workshop made already a grand show.

The King now came to Paris, and I went to pay him my respects. No sooner had his Majesty set eyes upon me than he called me cheerfully, and asked if I had something fine to exhibit at my lodging, for he would come to inspect it. I related all I had been doing; upon which he was seized with a strong desire to come. Accordingly, after his dinner, he set off with Madame de Tampes [Madame d'Étampes], the Cardinal of Lorraine, and some other of his greatest nobles, among whom were the King of Navarre, his cousin, and the Queen, his sister; the Dauphin and Dauphiness also attended him; so that upon that day the very flower of the French court came to visit me. I had been some time at home, and was hard at work. When the King arrived at the door of the castle and heard our hammers going, he bade his company keep silence. Everybody in my house was busily employed, so that the unexpected entrance of his Majesty took me by surprise. The first thing he saw on coming into the great hall was myself with a huge plate of silver in my hand, which I was beating for the body of my Jupiter; one of my men was finishing the head, another the legs; and it is easy to imagine what a din we made between us. It happened that a little French lad was working at my side, who had just been guilty of some trifling blunder. I gave the lad a kick, and, as my good luck would have it, caught him with my foot exactly in the fork between his legs, and sent him spinning several yards, so that he came stumbling up against the King precisely at the moment when his Majesty arrived. The King was vastly amused, but I felt covered with confusion. He began to ask me what I was engaged upon, and told me to go on working; then he said that he would much rather have me not employ my strength on manual labour, but take as many men as I wanted, and make them do the rough work; he should like me to keep myself in health, in order that he might enjoy my services through many years to come. I replied to his Majesty that the moment I left off working I should fall ill; and that my art itself would suffer, and not attain the mark I aimed at for his Majesty.

The Autobiography of Benvenuto Cellini, edited and abridged by Charles Hope. Oxford: Phaidon, 1983, p. 125.

DOCUMENT 16   **FRANCIS I: A CONTEMPORARY VIEW, 1546**

This description is by Marino Cavalli, Venetian ambassador to France.

The king is now fifty-four years old[1]: his appearance is quite regal, so that even without having his face or his portrait, simply by looking at him, one says immediately: 'this is the king'. His movements are so noble and majestic that no prince can equal him. His character is sturdy, in spite of the excessive fatigues which he has always endured and still endures in so many expeditions and journeys. Very few men could have supported such great adversities. Furthermore he purges himself of all the unwholesome humours that he might accumulate by a method which nature provides for him once a year: this may allow him to live for a very long time yet. He eats and drinks a great deal; sleeps even better and, what is more, he thinks only of leading a gay life. He is careful about his dress, which is full of braids and trimmings, rich in precious stones and ornaments; even his doublets are woven with gold thread; his shirt is of fine quality and comes out through the doublet's opening in accordance with French fashion. This delicate and choice way of life doubtless helps to preserve his health ... If the king endures bodily fatigues unflinchingly, he finds mental preoccupations more difficult to bear and hands them over almost entirely to the cardinal of Tournon and the admiral. He takes no decision and gives no reply without first listening to their advice: in all things he follows their counsel; and if ever (which is very rare) a reply is made to an ambassador or a concession which these two councillors have not approved, he cancels or modifies it. But in all the great matters of state, matters of peace or war, his Majesty, who is submissive in everything else, insists on his will being obeyed. In this event there is no one at court, however great his authority, who dares remonstrate with his Majesty. This prince has a sound judgement and wide learning; there is no object, study or art on which he cannot argue pertinently or judge with as much assurance as a specialist. His knowledge is not confined simply to the art of war ... he understands not only all that concerns naval warfare but is also very experienced in hunting, painting, literature, languages and the different bodily exercises appropriate to a good knight. Truly, when one sees that in spite of his knowledge and fine speeches, all his martial exploits have failed, one says that all his wisdom is on his lips, not in his mind. But I believe that the adversities of this prince are due to the lack of men able to carry out well his designs.

Relations des ambassadeurs vénitiens, [15], I, pp. 279–87.

[1]He was, in fact, fifty-two.

DOCUMENT 17 THE PALACE REVOLUTION, APRIL 1547

The following excerpt is from a dispatch sent by Jean de Saint-Mauris, imperial ambassador at the French court, to Charles V's chief minister, Granvelle.

On the penultimate day of March[1] the king died at Rambouillet of a fever that had lasted thirty days ... Two days before he died Madame d'Étampes left Rambouillet and went to her house at Limours. On the day after the king's death the dauphin and his wife went to a monastery near Rambouillet and the next day the dauphin was at Saint-Germain ...

On the same day as the dauphin was at Saint-Germain the constable [i.e. Anne de Montmorency] arrived there and was warmly welcomed by him. They spoke together in private for more than two hours. It is said that on the same night Longueval lost his offices and his lieutenancy of Champagne. The next day, Bayart, who was at court, was dismissed and stripped of his functions. He has retired to his house in a shocked state and it is reported that charges are being drawn up against him.

While the admiral [i.e. Annebault] is at Rambouillet, his marshalship has been given away, but as yet the recipient is unknown. He shall remain admiral but without his wages ... and he shall lose his governorship of Normandy, which is intended for Monsieur d'Aumale. It is said that Monsieur de Hesdin will be marshal of France and his wife is already lady-in-waiting to the new queen. The cardinal of Tournon has lost everything, and the count of Montrevel and the *sieur* de Grignan, his nephews, have been deprived of their governorships of Provence and Bresse. Rumour has it that Polin will lose command of the galleys, which will go to Piero Strozzi.

Saint-Ciergue and all the other knights of the order [of St Michael] who were members of the Privy Council, have been dismissed. Its president in judicial matters remains Monsieur de Reims [i.e. Charles de Guise, archbishop of Rheims] under the supervision of the constable, who wanted him as a companion, as he is of princely birth and in the past he has been accused of trying to do everything himself also to please *Sylvius* [i.e. Diane de Poitiers] who arranged his return to court.

The receivers of Sens and Marchaumont have been made secretaries of the said Council, and it is said that l'Aubespine will not come back. Bochetel is still there. The chancellor [i.e. François Olivier] is still dealing with business but is afraid of being dismissed: it is likely, however, that he will stay.

On the third of this month Madame d'Étampes sent one of her servants to ask for her usual lodging at Saint-Germain so that she might take leave of the dauphin. He told her servant that he should take his request to the queen and that he would do whatever she decided, letting her [Madame d'Étampes] understand that she had behaved very badly in causing her Majesty to be so ill treated. Already there are many people at court with complaints, who list the places she has taken from them; they will be heard and well provided for. No deceits are being used in dealing with the said lady or others people wish to harm: they are simply expelled and the dauphin says he does not want to hear anyone speak about the said Madame d'Étampes ...

Today the constable occupies the apartment coveted by the said Madame d'Étampes, and with him is the cardinal of Châtillon. Also the *sieurs* of Reims and Guise have been admitted to the king's household. The cardinal of Lorraine is always welcome and the cardinal of Ferrara is reasonably well considered, but the cardinal of Châtillon is becoming his rival. In short, this court is a new world, where no one has a good word for the policies of the cardinal of Tournon and the admiral towards the Protestants, the English and others ...

Printed in Castan, A., 'La mort de François Ier', *Mémoires de la société d'émulation du Doubs*, 5th series, iii (1878), pp. 445–50.

[1]Francis I died, in fact, on 31 March.

DOCUMENT 18 THE CONSTABLE OF MONTMORENCY

If he was a great trouncer of people, this was natural to him, for he had seen, done and remembered so much that when mistakes were made or someone tripped up in front of him, he knew how to correct them, using all the best arguments. Ah! how he would dress down his captains, both great and small, when they failed in their duty or tried to show off and dared to answer back! You may be sure that he made them eat humble pie, and not only them but also men of every condition, such as those gentlemen the presidents, councillors and men of law, when they had blundered. The least quality which he accorded them was to call them asses, oafs, fools, and [to say] that they thought themselves important, yet were only fatheads ...

Throughout his life he carefully observed his Christian faith and never strayed from it, failing neither in his devotions nor in his prayers. He said his prayers each day without fail, whether he was at home or riding with his men on campaign. They used to say that one should beware of the constable's prayers, for, as he muttered them, he would say according to circumstances: 'Go hang so-and-so! Tie him to a tree! Run him through with pikes or shoot him with arquebuses in front of me anon! Cut to pieces these rascals who have tried to hold this belfry against the king! Burn this village! Set fire to everything for a quarter of a league all round!' He would hand out such commands as were appropriate without breaking off his prayers, for he was so conscientious that he would have thought it a great fault to put them off till later.

Brantôme, [4], III, p. 295.

DOCUMENT 19   THE CHAMBRE ARDENTE, JULY 1548

A decree of 31 July 1548.

The court having examined the trial carried out by the *bailli* of Sens or his lieutenant of Robert le Lièvre, called Séraphin d'Argence, otherwise called Antoine Deschamps; Jehan Thuillier, called le Camus, instrument-player; Michiel Mareschal and Jehan Camus, spur-maker and prisoner in the *conciergerie* of the palace, on account of their crimes of heretical blasphemy ... the Court has sentenced and sentences Robert le Lièvre, as principal offender, to be imprisoned in the *conciergerie* and placed on a hurdle and dragged from the *conciergerie* to the place Maubert, and the said Thuillier, Mareschal and Jehan Camus to be placed each in a tumbril in front of the hurdle and also led to the place Maubert, where four gibbets shall be erected, the first of which shall be taller than the others by one foot; on to which the said le Lièvre, called Séraphin, principal author of the crimes and offences, shall be lifted and on to the other three shall also be lifted the said Thuillier, Mareschal and Jehan le Camus. And around each gibbet and at the same time a large fire shall be lit, and the prisoners shall be burned alive and their bodies consumed and reduced to ashes ... And the said court has declared and declares that all and each of the goods of the said prisoners are confiscated for the king.

Pronounced before the said prisoners on 1 August 1548.

And the court keeps in mind [*in mente curia*] that if the said prisoners should persist in their errors after the said decree has been pronounced, then, as soon as they begin to blaspheme against the honour and reverence of the Catholic faith, each shall have his tongue cut off. And should they not persist and should they demonstrate their true conversion to the holy Catholic church, then the said Thuillier, le Mareschal and Jehan Camus shall be strangled after feeling the fire a little.

Printed in Weiss, [119], p. 171.

DOCUMENT 20   AFFRAY IN THE RUE SAINT-JACQUES,
SEPTEMBER 1557

On 4 September between three and four hundred people of every quality gathered at nightfall in a house of the rue Saint-Jacques, opposite the collège du Plessis and behind the Sorbonne, to celebrate the Lord's supper. They were seen by some priests, students of the college, who had been watchful for some time after they had noticed an unusual crowd of people assembling there from time to time. They collected together as many of their faction as possible, sent a warning to the town watch and themselves did whatever they thought necessary to catch the said company ... The plan of these murderers was to do everything possible to prevent anyone leaving the house before the town watch had time to force its way into it. They had [collected] a large number of stones at their windows, enough to demolish a wall, with which to drive back those who would seek to leave [the house]. They began to carry out their cruel purpose at midnight as the poor people were about to go home. They attacked the exit to the house with an incredible fury and at the same time cried out loudly so as to attract support from all parts. In order to win over the people more effectively they claimed that those who had gathered there were thieves, brigands, and conspirators against the kingdom. Hearing this noise, the nearest person, on waking up, passed the signal to those further away, as is done in a public emergency, so that very soon the whole district was up in arms. For since the fall of Saint-Quentin the people had been continually subject to fears and alarms, and they had been ordered to provide themselves with weapons and be prepared. So each took up arms and rushed to the place whence the noise was coming. On discovering that they [i.e. the people inside the house] were not thieves, but Lutherans (they were still being called thus) they fell into an extreme rage and cried only for blood ... The danger that had sprung up so suddenly and unexpectedly caused great fear among those in the house, who thought they would be massacred within the hour. But those who guided and governed the church reassured them as far as possible ... One of two choices faced them: either to await the arrival of the magistrates and certain death by openly confessing their faith, or to break through the furious mob besieging the house. In the end, they were persuaded to break out by those familiar with the cowardice of the Parisian mob; it was decided that the men who carried swords would lead the way and fray a passage for the rest. The majority did this and many fled by various exits, avoiding such an infinite number of perils that it is a wonder any of them was able to get home safely ... Out of the whole group only one was struck by a stone as he found his way barred. He fell to the ground and was beaten up so mercilessly that he lost all human shape; he was then taken to the Benedictine cloister and exposed to public outrages. After several sallies had been made, only the women and young children remained inside the house, except for a few men who had been too scared to follow the rest. Some of them, however, threw themselves into neighbouring gardens where they were held until the magistrates arrived, while others, who tried to flee at dawn, were detained by the people after they had been badly beaten up and injured. The women, finding that their slender hope of protection by the men had vanished, decided to appear at the windows and beg for mercy, as the mob attacked the house with the aim of breaking in and sacking everything. Pleading innocence, the women asked for justice in accordance with the normal processes of the law. But all reason had deserted the furious populace ...

Bèze, [3], I, pp. 73–5.

DOCUMENT 21   THE PEACE OF CATEAU-CAMBRÉSIS, APRIL 1559

After all these comings and goings, which lasted for more than two months, peace was signed to the great misfortune of the king principally and of his kingdom. For this peace led to the surrender of all the territories and conquests which Kings Francis and Henry had won. Nor were they insignificant, having been estimated as equivalent in size to a third of the kingdom. I have read in a book, written in Spanish, that the king had given up 198 fortresses that had been garrisoned by him. I leave each person to guess how many more were dependent on those. And after this loss the peace brought us the death of King Henry, about whom all of us who bear arms may truly say that God had given the best king to his soldiers who had ever commanded in this kingdom; as for his people, such was their love for him that none spared the means to help him fight all the wars he had to cope with. I do not wish to blame those who made the peace, for it can be imagined that their motivation was good, and that they would never have made it if they had known that it would bring so many misfortunes; for they were such good servants of the king and loved him so much with good and just reason that they would rather have died in prison than make it. I say this because monsieur the constable was the prime mover along with monsieur the marshal of Saint-André. They themselves have witnessed the king's death, have shared in the calamities that have befallen this wretched kingdom and have died sword in hand. They might still be alive today. Thus one may judge that they did not make that peace with any thought for the misfortunes that it has occasioned.

Monluc, [12], II, pp. 376–7.

DOCUMENT 22   HENRY II: A CONTROVERSIAL MONARCH

The king's death gave rise to contradictory judgements and speeches. Some said that this prince deserved immortal praise: that, being bellicose and nearly always fortunate in war, he had extended the frontiers of France by subjugating a large part of Italy, conquering Scotland and the island of Corsica and transforming the two seas into a rampart for his kingdom; that, having routed Charles V at the battle of Renty, he had driven him into solitary retirement, oppressed by a greatness which he could see declining. They added that this king, who had always treated the Holy See with filial respect, had resumed the war to extricate Paul IV from embarrassment, and that he had brought back his troops from Italy only after Philip king of Spain and Mary queen of England had joined forces to attack France; that he had concluded a disadvantageous and dishonourable peace, but one that was at least useful to his subjects, and had assured public peace by marrying off his daughter and sister; finally, that the king, the best and most generous ever known, had died exercising his arms and universally mourned.

Others, on the contrary, declared that this prince, who had been fortunate in the early years of his reign, had spoilt the glory that he had gained in war by breaking the truce. Yet they admitted that it was less his fault than that of his bad advisers, who had led him into a disastrous conflict. They added that this enterprise had exhausted the [kingdom's] finances and sapped the strength of the nation, that battles had been lost whose memory still shamed the French, that this king and the great men of the state had been pawns of the ambition and perfidiousness of the Carafas; that the name of Frenchman had been virtually extinguished in Italy; that those who had escaped death in battle had since died of hunger and that few had returned to France; that in truth peace, which is always to be desired, had been obtained, but on shameful terms, and that the marriages of the princesses had been stipulated merely as a cover for its ignominy; finally, that this prince had died like a mere soldier in the midst of games and tournaments, showing off to his subjects. Nor were the private deeds of this prince overlooked: as a married man, he had taken a mistress, who had, as it were, bewitched him with her spells and become sole ruler. This, it was alleged, had given rise to a prodigious luxury, to the squandering of money, to shameful debaucheries and to the insatiable avarice of courtiers. And, talking of this corrupt century, one ought not to forget the large number of French poets whom he fathered. Abusing their talents, these poets flattered a vain woman with their shameful eulogies, diverted young men from serious and useful study into reading obscene verses, and corrupted the minds and hearts of the weaker sex by their licentious songs.

As for us, whose duty it is to judge impartially, we shall simply say that Henry loved war and, rejecting the wise counsels which Montmorency gave him from time to time in favour of peace, seized with joy every opportunity of taking up arms. Otherwise he was kind and easy-going and tended to follow the ideas of others rather than his own sentiments. Those who thought of the future believed that his death would be fatal to France. They foresaw that, as Henry would be leaving behind only infant princes, an ambitious mother who wanted to govern and a court divided by factions, peace would not last long, and that domestic strife would soon be followed by foreign wars, unless the sickness were quickly remedied.

Thou, J.–A, De, *Histoire universelle*, London, 1734, III, pp. 367–9.

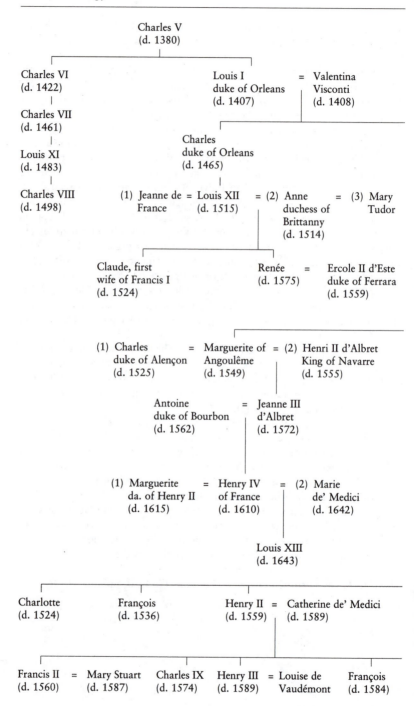

The House of Valois

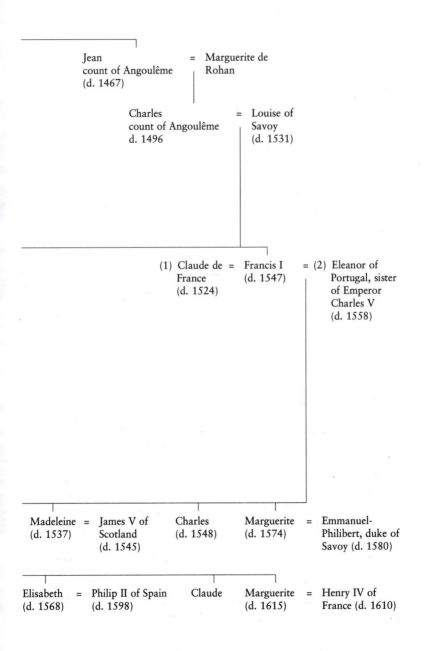

Jean count of Angoulême (d. 1467) = Marguerite de Rohan

Charles count of Angoulême d. 1496 = Louise of Savoy (d. 1531)

(1) Claude de France (d. 1524) = Francis I (d. 1547) = (2) Eleanor of Portugal, sister of Emperor Charles V (d. 1558)

Madeleine (d. 1537) = James V of Scotland (d. 1545)

Charles (d. 1548)

Marguerite (d. 1574) = Emmanuel-Philibert, duke of Savoy (d. 1580)

Elisabeth (d. 1568) = Philip II of Spain (d. 1598)

Claude

Marguerite (d. 1615) = Henry IV of France (d. 1610)

GLOSSARY

Aides A range of indirect taxes, mainly on wine.

Aisés The upper level of urban society: the well-to-do.

Arrêt A formal judgement pronounced by a court.

Aumône-générale A municipal system of poor relief, as at Lyons.

Aventuriers French volunteer infantrymen.

Bailliage The basic unit of royal administration at the local level, administered by the *bailli*.

Ban-et-arrière-ban The feudal levy.

Bureau des pauvres A secular department for poor relief.

Censier A written record of a tenant's obligations to his lord.

Chambre ardente The popular name for the chamber of the *parlement* created in 1547 to try cases of heresy.

Château A royal palace or aristocratic country house as distinct from a castle or *château-fort*.

Compagnies d'ordonnance The armoured cavalry of *gens d'armes* (hence its other name, *gendarmerie*), in which the nobility of sword served.

Confraternity An association of masters and artisans formed to celebrate the feast of a trade's patron saint and to participate in religious and public ceremonies.

Conseil des affaires The inner ring of the king's council; also called *conseil secret*.

Conseil d'état The king's council in its widest form.

Constable of France The highest military officer under the king.

Cornice A projecting ornamental moulding along the top of a building.

Crue A direct tax additional to the *taille* or *taillon*.

Curia regis The royal court in the early Middle Ages before some of its components (e.g. the *Parlement*) detached themselves from it and settled permanently in Paris.

Décharge A royal warrant authorising a payment.

Décime A tax levied by the clergy on all of its members for the purpose of paying a *don gratuit* (free gift) to the king.

Doléances Complaints submitted to the king by a representative body.

Douane A customs house.

Échevin An alderman in a municipal government.

Écu A gold crown. In 1515 it was worth 36 *sous* 3 *deniers*, or about 4 English shillings.

Élections Courts responsible for the local administration of the *taille* and other taxes; also the areas with which they dealt. The officials in charge were called *élus*.

Épargne Central treasury founded by Francis I in 1523. Its full name is *Trésor de l'Épargne*.

Estates-General The national representative body comprising elected representatives of the three orders of clergy, nobility and third estate.

Évocation The process whereby the king transferred a lawsuit from one court to another or to his council.

Finances extraordinaires The king's extraordinary revenue, drawn from taxation.

Finances ordinaires The king's ordinary revenue, drawn mainly from his demesne.

Gabelle A salt tax levied on a varying basis in five of six areas of France, the sixth being exempt.

Gallicanism A school of thought according to which the French church ought to be in certain respects free from papal control.

Gendarmerie Another name for the *compagnies d'ordonnance*.

Généralité Originally one of four fiscal areas, each one administered by a *général des finances*. In 1542 the *généralités* were sub-divided into sixteen *recettes-générales*, subsequently called *généralités* (as distinct from the *pays d'états*). As from 1552 they were run by officials called *trésoriers-généraux*.

Généraux des finances Senior officials who before 1523 administered the king's extraordinary revenues.

Gens des finances The collective name for the king's chief financial officials before 1523: the *généraux des finances* and *trésoriers de France*.

Gouvernement A provincial governorship.

Grand' chambre The principal chamber of the *parlement*.

Grand Conseil A judicial offshoot of the king's council. It became an independent sovereign court in 1497 but continued to follow the king on his travels.

Grands Jours Courts composed of magistrates from the *parlement* sitting in various provinces for a limited period.

Greek Cross A cross with four equal arms.

Grenier à sel A warehouse in which salt was kept, under the system of *gabelle*. The official in charge was a *grenetier*.

Herms Three-quarter-length figures on pedestals used as decorations in Renaissance architecture.

Humanism The programme of classical studies practised by certain scholars of the Renaissance (*humanists*) and the ideology stemming from that programme.

Iconoclasm The breaking of religious images.

Juges-délégués A special tribunal comprising two *parlementaires* and two theologians, set up in 1525 on the pope's authority to judge cases of heresy; abolished in 1527.

Landsknechts German mercenary infantry.

Langue d'oc The dialect spoken in southern France during the Middle Ages and in certain areas of the south till the nineteenth century.

Langue d'oïl Dialect spoken in northern France during the Middle Ages, the ancestor of modern French.

Lettre de jussion Royal command to the *parlement* demanding immediate and unqualified registration of legislation.

Lieutenant A local magistrate; also used to designate the deputy of a provincial governor.

Lit de justice Personal attendance of the king in the *parlement*, usually to enforce registration of legislation.

Livre The principal money of account in sixteenth-century France. 1 *livre* = 20 *sous*; 1 *sou* = 12 *deniers*; worth about 2 English shillings.

Loggia A gallery open on one or more sides, sometimes pillared.

Machicolation A projecting gallery built on the outside of a castle tower with openings in the floors through which boiling oil, missiles, etc. may be dropped on an enemy.

Maîtres des requêtes de l'hôtel Officials attached to the royal council and under the chancellor's control.

Menu peuple The lowest level of urban society, comprising manual workers and domestic servants.

Mnemonic Designed to aid memory.

Nominalism A school of thought regarding universals or abstract concepts as mere names, without any corresponding realities.

Office A permanent government post (as distinct from a commission, which was temporary). It was often sold and entailed some measure of ennoblement.

Order In classical architecture, a column with base (usually), shaft, capital and entablature, decorated and proportioned according to the Doric, Ionic, Corinthian or Composite mode.

Ordinance A law or edict.

Parlement The highest court of law under the king, also responsible for registering royal edicts and with administrative duties. Apart from the *Parlement* of Paris, there were seven provincial *parlements* (Aix-en Provence, Bordeaux, Dijon, Grenoble, Rennes, Rouen and Toulouse) which in theory were subordinate to it, but which in time acquired similar powers within their own provincial limits (*ressorts*).

Parlementaire Any magistrate serving in a *parlement*.

Parties casuelles A special treasury set up by Francis I to receive the proceeds from the sale of office.

Pays d'élections Provinces in which taxation was levied by the *élus* on orders from the council, i.e. most of France.

Pays d'états Provinces in which taxation was levied by the local estates (e.g. Languedoc, Brittany, Burgundy and Provence) as distinct from the *pays d'élections*, where taxation was levied by officials called *élus*, on orders from the council.

Pediment In classical architecture, a low-pitched gable, straight-sided or curved, above a portico, door or window.

Pilaster A shallow pier or rectangular column projecting only slightly from a wall.

Portcullis A reinforced gate made to slide up and down in the vertical jambs of a doorway used for defence in castle gateways.

Premier président The presiding magistrate in a *parlement*.

Présidiaux Courts set up in 1552 between the provincial *parlements* and the *bailliage* courts.

Prévôt de l'hôtel Official in charge of keeping law and order in the royal court.

Prévôt des marchands The mayor of Paris.

Procureur A solicitor. In every royal court there was a *procureur du roi*, known in the *parlement* as the *procureur-général*.

Putti Representations of nude children frequently used in Renaissance art.

Realism The scholastic doctrine of the objective or absolute existence of universals (abstract concepts), of which Thomas Aquinas (1225–74) was the chief exponent.

Receveur des parties casuelles See *Parties casuelles*.

Receveur ordinaire A receiver of royal revenue.

Remontrances (Remonstrances) Objections or grievances submitted to the king, verbally or in writing, by a *parlement*, usually in response to a legislative proposal.

Rente A government bond issued on the security of municipal revenues. A *rentier* was a person living off such an investment.

Sacramentarianism A body of Protestant thought, held mainly by Zwingli and his followers, which rejected the doctrine of the Real Presence of Christ in the Eucharist.

Sacre Literally, the consecration of a new French king; more loosely, his coronation.

Salic law One of the so-called fundamental laws of the French monarchy, whereby females were excluded from the succession to the throne.

Scholasticism The characteristic method of teaching in medieval universities. Also its Christian philosophy with its strong dependence on Aristotelian texts and commentaries. Almost synonymous with medieval, as distinct from Renaissance, thought.

Secrétaires des finances Officials who prepared and countersigned royal correspondence. From them evolved the four *secrétaires d'état* in 1547.

Seigneurie The basic economic unit in rural France. The obligations of tenants to the *seigneur* involved a complex of rights, services and dues. A *seigneur* enjoyed rights of jurisdiction of varying degrees (called 'high', 'middle' and 'low' according to the severity of the penalties prescribed) within his lands, albeit subject to appeal to a royal court.

Sénéchaussée Another name, used mainly in southern France, for a *bailliage*. The equivalent to a *bailli* was a *sénéchal*.

Setier A measurement of capacity.

Sorbonne The faculty of theology of the university of Paris.

Sou A unit of currency. 1 *sou* = 12 *deniers*.

Sovereign courts High courts, such as the *Parlement* of Paris, which had originally formed part of the king's court (*Curia Regis*).

Strapwork Decoration consisting of interlaced bands and forms similar to fretwork or cut leather.

Stucco Plasterwork.

Syndic A person chosen to look after the interests of a group or corporation, e.g. the *syndic* of the Sorbonne.

Taille The principal direct tax, levied in two ways: the *taille personnelle*, levied on the unprivileged in the north, and the *taille réelle*, levied on non-noble land in the south.

Taillon An addition to the *taille* introduced under Henry II.

Thaumaturgical Pertaining to the working of miracles, more specifically the healing of the sick.

Tournelle criminelle Chamber of criminal justice in the *parlement*.

Trésorier de l'Épargne See *Épargne*.

Trésoriers de France Four officials who before 1523 administered the king's ordinary revenues.

Vicomté In local government a jurisdiction below the *bailliage* and equivalent to a *prévôté*.

Ville-franche A town exempt from the *taille*.

BIBLIOGRAPHY

PRIMARY SOURCES: MANUSCRIPT

1 Archives nationales, Paris, Ms. X^{la} 1536, Register of the *Parlement* of Paris.

2 Archives nationales, Paris, Ms. X^{la} 1556, Register of the *Parlement* of Paris.

PRIMARY SOURCES: PRINTED

3 Bèze, T. de, *Histoire ecclésiastique des églises réformées au royaume de France*, Vol. 1. Lille, 1841.

4 Brantôme, P. de Bourdeille, abbé de, *Oeuvres complètes*, ed. L. Lalanne, 11 vols. Paris, 1864–82.

5 *Catalogue des actes de François Ier*, 10 vols. Paris, 1887–1910.

6 *Cronique du roy Françoys Premier de ce nom*, ed. G. Guiffrey. Paris, 1860.

7 Isambert, F.-A., *Receuil général des anciennes lois françaises*, 29 vols. Paris, 1827–33.

8 *Journal de Jean Barrillon, secrétaire du chancelier Duprat, 1515–21*, ed. P. de Vaissière, 2 vols. Paris, 1897–99.

9 *Journal d'un bourgeois de Paris sous le règne de François Ier, 1515–1536*, ed. V.-L. Bourrilly. Paris, 1910.

10 *The Life of Benvenuto Cellini Written by Himself*, trans. J.A. Symonds, ed. J. Pope-Hennessy. London: Phaidon, 1949.

11 *Mémoires de Martin et Guillaume du Bellay*, ed. V.-L. Bourrilly and F. Vindry, 4 vols. Paris, 1908–19.

12 Monluc, Blaise de, *Commentaires*, ed. P. Courteault, 3 vols. Paris, 1911–25.

13 *Ordonnances des rois de France: règne de François Ier*, 9 vols. Paris, 1902–75. In continuation.

14 *Le Prince dans la France des XVIe et XVIIe siècles*, ed. C. Bontems, L.-P. Raybaud and J.-P. Brancourt. Paris, 1965.

15 *Relations des ambassadeurs vénitiens sur les affaires de France*, ed. N. Tommaseo, 2 vols. Paris, 1838.

16 Seyssel, Claude de, *The Monarchy of France*, trans. J. H. Hexter, ed. D. R. Kelley. New Haven and London: Yale University Press, 1981.

SECONDARY SOURCES: BOOKS

17   Armstrong, Elizabeth, *Robert Estienne, Royal Printer*, Revised edition. Sutton Courtenay Press, 1986.
18   Audisio, G., *Les Vaudois du Luberon. Une minorité en Provence (1460–1560)*. Mérindol, 1984.
19   Babelon, J.-P., *Paris au XVIe siècle*. Paris, 1986.
20   Babelon, J.-P., *Châteaux de France au siècle de la Renaissance*. Paris, 1989.
21   Baumgartner, F. C., *Henry II King of France, 1547–1559*. Durham, NC, 1988.
22   Baumgartner, F. C., *Louis XII*. Stroud: Alan Sutton, 1994.
23   Beaune, Colette, *The Birth of an Ideology: Myths and Symbols of Nation in Late-Medieval France*. Berkeley, CA, 1991.
24   Béguin, Sylvie, *L'École de Fontainebleau: Le maniérisme à la cour de France*. Paris, 1960.
25   Béguin, Sylvie, Guillaume, J., and Roy, A., *La Galerie d'Ulysse à Fontainebleau*. Paris, 1985.
26   Benedict, P., *Rouen during the Wars of Religion*. Cambridge: Cambridge University Press, 1981.
27   Benedict, P., (ed.), *Cities and Social Change in Early Modern France*. London, Unwin Hyman, 1989.
28   Berthoud, G., *Antoine Marcourt*. Geneva, 1973.
29   Bloch, M., *The Royal Touch: Sacred Monarchy and Scrofula in England and France*. London: Routledge and Kegan Paul, 1973.
30   Blunt, A., *Art and Architecture in France, 1500–1700*. Harmondsworth: Penguin, 1957.
31   Blunt, A., *Philibert de L'Orme*. London: Zwemmer, 1958.
32   Bourrilly, V.–L., *Guillaume du Bellay*. Paris, 1905.
33   Brandi, K., *The Emperor Charles V*. London: Cape, 1939.
34   Bryant, L. M., *The King and the City in the Parisian Royal Entry Ceremony: Politics, Ritual and Art in the Renaissance*. Geneva, 1986.
35   Buisson, A., *Le Chancelier Antoine Duprat*. Paris, 1935.
36   Caroll, E. A., 'Rosso in France', in *Actes du colloque international sur l'art de Fontainebleau*, ed. A. Chastel. Paris, 1975.
37   Charton-Le Clech, Sylvie, *Chancellerie et culture au XVIe siècle (les notaires et secrétaires du roi de 1515 à 1547)*. Toulouse, 1993.
38   Chartrou, J., *Les entrées solennelles et triomphales à la Renaissance (1484–1551)*. Paris, 1928.
39   Chatenet, Monique, *Le Château de Madrid au bois de Boulogne*. Paris, 1987.
40   Chaunu, P. and Gascon, R., *Histoire économique et sociale de la France, I (1450–1660)*, Pt 1: *L'État et la ville*. Paris, 1977.
41   Chevalier, B., *Les bonnes villes de France du XIVe au XVIe siècle*. Paris, 1982.

42   Church, W. F., *Constitutional Thought in Sixteenth-Century France.*
      Cambridge, MA, 1941.
43   Cloulas, I., *Catherine de Médicis.* Paris, 1979.
44   Cloulas, I., *Henri II.* Paris, 1985.
45   Constant, J.–M., *Les Guise.* Paris, 1984.
46   Constant, J.–M,. *De la noblesse française aux XVIe–XVIIe siècles.*
      Paris, 1985.
47   Contamine, P., (ed.), *Histoire militaire de la France: Des Origines à*
      1715. Paris, 1992.
48   Croix, A., *Nantes et le pays nantais au XVIe siècle.* Paris, 1974.
49   Davis, N. Z., *Society and Culture in Early Modern France.* London:
      Duckworth, 1975.
50   Decrue, F., *Anne de Montmorency,* 2 vols. Paris, 1885–89.
51   Dognon, P., *Les Institutions politiques et administratives du pays de*
      Languedoc du XIIIe siècle aux Guerres de Religion. Toulouse,
      1895.
52   Doucet, R., *Étude sur le gouvernement de François Ier dans ses*
      rapports avec le Parlement de Paris, 2 vols. Paris and Algiers,
      1921–26.
53   Doucet, R., *Les Institutions de la France au XVIe siècle,* 2 vols.
      Paris, 1948.
54   Duby, G. and Wallon, A. (eds), *Histoire de la France rurale,* Vol. 2.
      Paris, 1975.
55   *L'École de Fontainebleau.* Catalogue of exhibition at the Grand
      Palais, Paris, 1972.
56   Farge, J. K., *Orthodoxy and Reform in Early Reformation France.*
      Leiden, 1985.
57   Febvre, L., *Au coeur religieux du XVIe siècle.* Paris, 1957.
58   Floquet, A., *Histoire du parlement de Normandie,* 7 vols. Rouen, 1840.
59   François, M., *Le Cardinal François de Tournon.* Paris, 1951.
60   Franklin, J.H., *Jean Bodin and the Rise of Absolutist Theory.*
      Cambridge: Cambridge University Press, 1973.
61   Gascon, R., *Grand Commerce et vie urbaine au XVIe siècle: Lyon et*
      ses marchands, 2 vols. Paris, 1971.
62   Giesey, R., *The Royal Funeral Ceremony in Renaissance France.*
      Geneva, 1960.
63   Gigon, S.–C., *La révolte de la gabelle en Guyenne, 1548–1549.* Paris,
      1906.
64   Goubert, P., 'Recent theories and research on French population
      between 1500–1700', in *Population in History,* ed. D. V. Glass and
      D. E. C. Eversley. London: Edward Arnold, 1965.
65   Greengrass, M., *The French Reformation.* Oxford: Blackwell, 1987.
66   Gutton, J.–P., *La Société et les pauvres: l'exemple de la généralité de*
      Lyon, 1534–1789. Paris, 1971.
67   Hamon, P., *L'Argent du roi. Les finances sous François Ier.* Paris,
      1994.

68 Harding, R. R., *Anatomy of a Power Élite: The Provincial Governors in Early Modern France*. New Haven and London: Yale University Press, 1978.

69 Hari, R., 'Les placards de 1534', in *Aspects de la propagande religieuse*, ed. G. Berthoud et al. Geneva, 1957.

70 Heller, H., *The Conquest of Poverty. The Calvinist Revolt in Sixteenth Century France*. Leiden, 1986.

71 Heller, H., *Iron and Blood: Civil Wars in Sixteenth-Century France*. Montreal and Kingston: McGill-Queen's University Press, 1991.

72 Hobson, A., *Great Libraries*. London, 1970.

73 Hobson, A., *Humanists and Bookbinders*. Cambridge: Cambridge University Press, 1989.

74 Imbart de la Tour, P., *Les Origines de la Réforme*, 4 vols. Paris, 1905–35.

75 Jackson, R. A., *Vive le Roi! A History of the French Coronation from Charles V to Charles X*. Chapel Hill, NC: University of North Carolina Press, 1984.

76 Jacquart, J., *La crise rurale en Ile–de–France, 1550–1670*. Paris, 1974.

77 Jacquart, J., *Bayard*. Paris, 1987.

78 Jacquart, J., *François Ier*, 2nd edn. Paris, 1994.

79 Jacqueton, G., *La Politique extérieure de Louise de Savoie*. Paris, 1892.

80 Knecht, R. J., *Renaissance Warrior and Patron: The Reign of Francis I*. Cambridge: Cambridge University Press, 1994.

81 Lecoq, Anne–Marie, *François Ier imaginaire: Symbolique et politique à l'aube de la Renaissance française*. Paris 1987.

82 Le Roy Ladurie, E. and Morineau, M., *Histoire économique et sociale de la France, I (1450–1660), Pt 2: Paysannerie et croissance*. Paris, 1977.

83 Lloyd, Howell A., *The State, France and the Sixteenth Century*. London: Allen and Unwin, 1993.

84 Lot, F., *Recherches sur les effectifs des armées françaises des Guerres d'Italie aux Guerres de Religion, 1494–1562*. Paris, 1962.

85 Major, J. Russell, *Representative Institutions in Renaissance France, 1421–1559*. Madison WI: University of Wisconsin Press, 1960.

86 Major, J. Russell, *Representative Government in Early Modern France*. New Haven and London: Yale University Press, 1980.

87 Major, J. Russell, *From Renaissance Monarchy to Absolute Monarchy: French Kings, Nobles and Estates*. Baltimore, MD, 1994.

88 Mann, M., *Érasme et les débuts de la réforme française, 1517–1536*. Paris, 1934.

89 Maugis, E., *Histoire du Parlement de Paris*, 3 vols. Paris, 1913–16.

90 McGowan, Margaret M., *Ideal Forms in the Age of Ronsard*. Berkeley, CA: University of California Press, 1985.

91 McNeil, D. O., *Guillaume Budé and Humanism in the Reign of Francis I*. Geneva, 1975.

92   Mellen, P., *Jean Clouet*. London: Phaidon, 1971.
93   Michelet, J., *Histoire de France*, Vols. 9, 10. Paris, no date.
94   Mousnier, R., *La Vénalité des offices sous Henri IV et Louis XIII*. 2nd edn. Paris, 1971.
95   Nicholls, D., 'France', in *The Early Reformation in Europe*, ed. A. Pettegree. Cambridge: Cambridge University Press, 1992.
96   Pagès, G., *La Monarchie d'ancien régime en France*. Paris, 1946.
97   Parker, D., *The Making of French Absolutism*. London: Edward Arnold, 1983.
98   Parker, T. H. L., *John Calvin*. London: Dent, 1975.
99   Pope–Hennessy, J., *Cellini*. London: Macmillan, 1985.
100 Potter, D., *War and Government in the French Provinces. Picardy, 1470–1560*. Cambridge: Cambridge University Press, 1993.
101 Potter, D., *A History of France, 1460–1560. The Emergence of a Nation State*. London, 1995.
102 Prentout, H., *Les États provinciaux de Normandie*, 3 vols. Caen, 1925.
103 Quilliet, B., *Louis XII, Père du Peuple*. Paris, 1986.
104 Romier, L., *Les Origines politiques des Guerres de Religion*, 2 vols. Paris, 1913–14.
105 Russell, J. G., *The Field of Cloth of Gold*. London: Routledge, 1969.
106 Scailliérez, Cécile, *François Ier et ses artistes dans les collections du Louvre*. Paris, 1992.
107 Scarisbrick, J. J., *Henry VIII*. London: Eyre and Spottiswoode, 1968.
108 Schick, L., *Un Grand Homme d'affaires au début du XVIe siècle: Jacob Fugger*. Paris, 1957.
109 Schnapper, B., *Les Rentes au XVIe siècle*. Paris, 1957.
110 Screech, M.A., *Rabelais*. London: Duckworth, 1979.
111 Shennan, J.H., *The Parlement of Paris*. London : Eyre and Spottiswoode, 1968.
112 Skinner, Q., *The Foundations of Modern Political Thought*. 2 vols. Cambridge: Cambridge University Press, 1978.
113 Smith, Pauline M., *Clément Marot, Poet of the French Renaissance*. London: The Athlone Press, 1970
114 Spont, A., *Semblançay (?–1527) : La bourgeoisie financière au début du XVIe siècle*. Paris, 1985.
115 Sutherland, N. M., *The Huguenot Struggle for Recognition*. New Haven and London: Yale University Press, 1980.
116 Ursu, J., *La Politique orientale de François Ier*. Paris, 1908.
117 Veissière, M., *L'evêque Guillaume Briçonnet (1470–1534)*. Provins, 1986.
118 Venard, M., *Réforme protestante, Réforme catholique dans la province d'Avignon, XVIe siècle*. Paris, 1993.
119 Weiss, N., *La Chambre ardente*. Paris, 1889.
120 Wendel, F., *Calvin*. London: Collins, 1965.
121 Wolfe, M., *The Fiscal System of Renaissance France*. New Haven and London: Yale University Press, 1972.

122 Yates, F., *The French Academies of the Sixteenth Century*. London: Routledge, 1988.

123 Zeller, G., *La Réunion de Metz à la France*, 2 vols. Paris, 1926.

124 Zeller, G., *Les Institutions de la France au XVIe siècle*. Paris, 1948.

125 Zerner, H., *The School of Fontainebleau: Etchings and Engravings*. London: Thames and Hudson, 1969

ARTICLES

The following abbreviations are used:

AUP	*Annales de l'Université de Paris*
BHJ	*Birmingham Historical Journal*
BIHR	*Bulletin of the Institute of Historical Research*
BSHPF	*Bulletin de la société de l'histoire du protestantisme français*
EHR	*English Historical Review*
ESR	*European Studies Review*
FH	*French History*
FHS	*French Historical Studies*
H	*History*
HJ	*Historical Journal*
PAPS	*Proceedings of the American Philosophical Society*
RA	*Revue de l'Art*
REP	*Revue d'économie politique*
RFHIP	*Revue française d'histoire des idées politiques*
RH	*Revue historique*
SCJ	*Sixteenth-Century Journal*

126 Bourrilly, V.-L. and Weiss, N., 'Jean du Bellay, les Protestants et la Sorbonne', *BSHPF*, lii (1903), pp. 97–127, 193–231; liii (1904), pp. 97–143.

127 Cauwès, P., 'Les commencements du crédit public en France: les rentes sur l'hôtel de ville au XVIe siècle', *REP*, ix (1895), pp. 97–123.

128 Chatenet, Monique, 'Une demeure royale au milieu du XVIe siècle: La distribution des espaces au château de Saint-Germain-en-Laye', *RA*, 81 (1988), pp. 20–30.

129 Coornaert, E., 'La politique économique de la France au début du règne de François Ier', *AUP*, viii (1933), pp. 414–27.

130 Doucet, R., 'Le Grand Parti de Lyon au XVIe siècle', *RH*, clxxi (1933), pp. 474–82.

131 Guillaume, J., 'Léonard de Vinci et l'architecture française', *RA*, 25 (1974), pp. 71–91.

132 Gwyn, P., 'Wolsey's foreign policy: the conferences at Calais and Bruges reconsidered', *HJ*, 23 (1980), pp. 755–72.

133   Hamon, P., 'L'Honneur, l'argent et la Bourgogne: La rançon de
      François Premier', *RFHIP*, 1 (1995), pp. 9–38.
134   Hauser, H., 'Le traité de Madrid et la cession de la Bourgogne à
      Charles-Quint', *Revue bourguignonne*, xxii (1912) No. 3.
135   Jacqueton, G., 'Le Trésor de l'Épargne sous François Ier, 1523–47',
      RH, lv (1894), pp. 1–43; lvi (1894), pp. 1– 38.
136   Knecht, R. J., 'The Concordat of 1516: a re-assessment', *BHJ*, ix
      (1963), pp. 16–32. Reprinted in *Government in Reformation
      Europe*, ed. H. J. Cohn. London: Macmillan, 1971, pp. 91–112.
137   Knecht, R. J., 'The Court of Francis I', *ESR*, viii (1978), pp. 1–22.
138   Knecht, R. J., 'Francis I and Paris', *H*, lxvi (1981), pp. 18–33.
139   Knecht, R. J., 'Francis I and the *lit de justice*: a "legend" defended',
      FH, 7 (1993), pp. 53–83.
140   Nicholls, D., 'Social change and early Protestantism in France:
      Normandy, 1520–62', *ESR*, 10 (1980), pp. 279–308.
141   Nicholls, D., 'The nature of popular heresy in France, 1520–1542',
      HJ, 26 (1983), pp. 261–75.
142   Potter, D. L., 'Foreign policy in the age of the Reformation: French
      involvement in the Schmalkaldic War', *HJ*, xx (1977), pp. 525–44.
143   Potter, D. L., 'The duc de Guise and the fall of Calais, 1557–58',
      EHR, 118 (1983), pp. 481–512.
144   Russell, J. G., 'The search for universal peace: the conferences at
      Calais and Bruges in 1521', *BIHR*, xliv (1971), pp. 162–93.
145   Stocker, C. W., 'The politics of the Parlement of Paris in 1525', *FHS*,
      viii (1973), pp. 191–212.
146   Stocker, C. W., 'Public and private enterprise in the administration of
      a Renaissance Monarchy: the first sales of offices in the Parlement
      of Paris (1512–24)', *SCJ*, ix (1978), pp. 4–29.
147   Van Doren, L. Scott, 'War taxation, institutional change and social
      conflict in provincial France: the royal *taille* in Dauphiné,
      1494–1559', *PAPS*, cxxi (1977), pp. 70–96.

INDEX

absolutism, 13–14, 16, 86, 94–5, 98
Agincourt, battle of, 36
agriculture, 6, 11
aides, 20–1
Aigues-Mortes, 41, 68
Aix-en-Provence, 40; *parlement* of, 2, 18, 69
Alba, Fernando Alvarez de Toledo (d.1531), 2nd duke of, viceroy of Naples, 44
Alberti, Leone Battista (1404–72), architect, 79
Albi, estates of, 93
Albret, house of, 1, 33
Albret, Jean d', king of Navarre, 32, 106, 112
Algiers, 42
Alluye, *seigneur* d', 104, 106
Amboise, 66, 80, 87
Amboise, *château* of, 65, 76
Amboise, Georges d' (1460–1515), archbishop of Rouen, cardinal, 76
Amiens, 4, 7; treaty of (1527), 36
Andelot, François d', 71
Anet, *château* of, 79, 81
Angers, 50
Angoulême, Charles (d. 1495), count of, 24
Anjou, house of, 31
Anna, niece of the Emperor Charles V, 42
Anne de France, (1460–1522), duchess of Bourbon, 3

Anne (1477–1514), duchess of Brittany (1488–1514), queen of France as from 1491, 2, 25
Annebault, Claude d' (d. 1552), admiral of France, 28, 92, 113–15
Antiquity, cult of, 82
Antwerp, 9
Aragon, 1, 31–2
house of, 30
architecture, 76
Ardres, treaty of (1546), 43
Aretino, Pietro (1492–1556), writer, 80–1
Aristotle, 59
Armagnac, Georges d', bishop of Rodez, 84
artisans, 7, 74
Artois, 1–2, 37
Aumale, *see* Guise, François de
Aumône-générale, 8
Auvergne, 17, 49
Auxonne, estates of, 89
aventuriers, 48

Babou, Philibert, first *Trésorier de l'Épargne,* 53
Bailli(s), 16, 89
Bailliage(s), 7, 16, 102
Baltic states, 9
Ban et arrière-ban, 16, 90
Bankers, 50, 55–6, 58
Bar, duchy of, 1
Bar-le-Duc, 39
Barbarossa, Khair-ad-Din (1467–1546), Algerian corsair, 39, 42

Barcelona, 39; treaty of (1529), 37
Barrillon, Jean, secretary to
    Cardinal Duprat, 97, 101, 103
Basel (Basle), 60
Batarnay, Ymbert de, *seigneur* du
    Bouchage, 50
Bayart, Gilbert, *secrétaire des*
    finances, 114
Bayeux, *Grands Jours* of (1540),
    92, 94
Beaujeu, Pierre de, 3
Beaune, Jacques de (d. 1527),
    baron of Semblançay, 26, 52–4,
    103–4
Béda, Noël (1470?–1537), syndic of
    the Sorbonne, 61
Belli, Valerio, (1468–1546), 81
Berquin, Louis de (d. 1529), writer,
    62–4
Berry, 9
Bèze, Théodore de (Theodore Beza)
    (1519–1605), theologian, 71, 98
Bibliothèque nationale, Paris, 85
Black Death, 5–6
Blois, 4, 76, 107; *château* of, 76
Bochetel, Guillaume, *secrétaire des*
    finances, 114
Bodin, Jean (1530–96), political
    writer, 56
Bohemia, king of, 34
Bois de Boulogne, 77
Boisy, Artus Gouffier (1475?–
    1519), *seigneur* de, 33, 50
Boleyn, Anne, queen of England, 38
Bologna, 32, 38; *see also*
    Concordat of Bologna
Bomy, truce of (1537), 40
Bonnivet, Admiral, *see* Gouffier,
    Guillaume
Bontemps, Pierre (1506?–70?),
    sculptor, 82
Bordeaux, 4, 6–7, 9, 75; *parlement*
    of, 2, 18, 102
Boulogne, 38, 42–3
Bourbon demesne, 1–3; house of, 3
Bourbon, Antoine de (1518–62),

duke of Vendôme, then king of
    Navarre (from 1555), 71–2
Bourbon, Charles (1490–1527), 3rd
    duke of, constable of France, 3,
    35–6, 40–1, 96
Bourbon, Suzanne de (d.1521), wife
    of Charles 3rd duke of Bourbon,
Bourbon-Montpensier, house of, 3
bourgeoisie, 21, 69
Bourges, archbishop of, 104, 106
Boyvin, René, engraver, 80
Bramante, Donato (1444–1514),
    architect, 76
Brandenburg, bishop of, 103;
    margrave of, 34, 102
Brantôme, Pierre de Bourdeille
    (1540–1614), *abbé* de, 98
Bresse, 114
Bresse, Philip, count of, 24
Brethren of the Common Life, 59
Briçonnet, Guillaume (1470–1534),
    bishop of Meaux, 60–1
Brittany, 18, 49, 90, 92; duchy of,
    1–3, 36; estates of, 3
Bruges, treaty of (1521), 35
Brussels, 44
Budé, Guillaume (1467–1540),
    humanist scholar, 83–4, 86
Burgundy, 31, 37, 49, 88, 92, 98;
    estates of, 88; house of, 1

Cabala, the, 83
Cabrières, 70
Calais, 1–3, 29, 35, 43, 45
Calvin, John (1509–64) reformer,
    65, 68–70, 72, 98
Calvinism, 67
Cambrai, 37, 43; peace of (1529),
    2, 26, 37–8, 55, 80; treaty of
    (1517), 33
Camillo, Giulio, 83
Camus, Jean, 116
Carafa, Carlo, cardinal, 44
Carafa, house of, 119
Caroli, Pierre, 60, 62–3, 65
Casa de Campo, Madrid, 77

Castile, 32, 44

Cateau-Cambrésis, peace of (1559), 29, 45, 58, 118

Catherine de' Medici (1519–89), queen of France, wife of Henry II, 12, 28, 38–9, 45, 79, 81, 112, 114, 119

Cavalli, Marino, Venetian ambassador, 113

Cellini, Benvenuto (1500–71), sculptor, goldsmith and engraver, 27, 75, 81–2, 112

censorship, 17, 62

Cercle de Meaux, 26, 60–1, 63–64

Chabot, Philippe (1480–1543), *seigneur* de Brion, admiral of France, 40, 88–9

Chalon, house of, 1

Chambiges, Pierre (d.1544) master-mason, 77

Chambord, *château* of, 77, 79; treaty of (1552), 43

Chambre ardente, 17, 70, 115

Champagne, 9, 49, 114

Champier, Symphorien, 107

Chancellor of France, 15; *see also* Duprat, Antoine; Olivier, François

chancery, 15

Chantilly, *château* of, 79

Charles III, duke of Savoy (1504–53), 40

Charles IX, king of France (1560–74), 24, 85, 89

Charles V, Holy Roman Emperor (1519–58), 4, 26, 30–2, 34–5, 39–42, 47, 55, 62, 68, 70, 83, 88–90, 103–5, 118

Charles V, king of France (1364–80), 21

Charles VII, king of France (1422–61), 2, 22, 57

Charles VIII, king of France (1483–98), 2, 25, 31, 76, 84

Charles, duke of Angoulême, then duke of Orleans, 3rd son of Francis I, 27, 40, 42–3

Château-Neuf (Saint-Germain-en-Laye), 79

Châteaubriand, edict of (1551), 70

Châtellerault, edict of (1541), 57

Châtillon, house of, 43

Châtillon, Odet de, cardinal, 71, 115

Cheney, Sir Thomas, 74

Cicero, 13

Claude de France (d. 1524), queen of France, 1st wife of Francis I, 2–3, 26

Clement VII (Giulio de' Medici), pope (1523–34), 36–39, 55, 63–4, 81

clergy, 7, 20, 50, 52, 55, 68–9, 93–4, 96

cloth, 7, 9–10

Clouet, François (1520–72), artist, 80, 82

Clouet, Jean (1475?–1541), artist, 80

Coblenz, 102

Cognac, 24, 88; edict of (1542), 56; Holy League of (1526), 36

coinage, 10, 50

Coligny, Gaspard de (d. 1572), admiral of France, 71

Collège de France, 84

Cologne, archbishop of, 34

Colonna, Prospero, 35

communications, 4

compagnies d'ordonnance, 19–20

Compiègne, edict of (1557), 70

Comtat-Venaissin, 1

Concordat of Bologna (1516), 32, 50, 86–8, 100

Condé, Louis de, 71

confraternities, 11

Constantinople, 33, 39

Cop, Guillaume, 83

Cop, Nicolas, 65–6

Corneille de Lyon (d.1574?), 82

coronation, 13, 61, 70

Correggio, Antonio Allegri da (1489–1534), painter, 82

Corsica, 45, 118

Coucy, edict of (1535), 67–8, 110
Council, King's, 12, 14–16, 19–20,
  22, 45, 52, 57, 86, 88–9, 93,
  101, 104, 106, 114
Court, 19, 22, 27, 39–40, 44, 64,
  73–5, 77, 81, 84–5, 87, 112,
  114–15, 119; cost of, 47
Crémieu, edict of (1536), 16
Cremona, 35–6
Crépy, peace of (1544), 2, 27, 42
Crown lands, alienation of, 50, 51–2
currency, *see* coinage
customs duties, 10
customs, codification of, 2

Dauphin *see* François, eldest son of
  Francis I, and Henry II
Dauphiné, 49, 60, 69, 90, 92
  estates of, 49
de l'Orme, Philibert (1510?–1570),
  architect, 79–80
De Thou, Jacques Auguste, lawyer
  and historian, 98
Décime(s), 47, 50, 55–6,
dell'Abbate, Niccolò
  (1509?–1571?), painter, 81–2
della Palla, Battista, 81
della Robbia, Girolamo
  (1488–1566), ceramist, 77
demesne (domain), royal, 16, 49,
  53, 99, 102
Demoulins, François, 83
Diane de Poitiers (1499–1566),
  mistress of Henry II, 28, 79, 81,
  114, 119
Dijon, 31, 88; *parlement* of, 18
Dolet, Étienne (1509–46),
  scholar-printer, 69
Doria, Andrea (1466–1560),
  Genoese admiral, 37
Doria, Filippino, 37
du Bellay, Guillaume, (1491–1543),
  seigneur de Langey, 38, 66, 80,
  97, 104
du Bellay, Jean (1492–1560),
  bishop of Paris, cardinal, 39, 79

du Bellay, Martin, 97, 104
du Bourg, Anne, 72
du Pléssis, *collège*, 116
Duprat, Antoine, chancellor of
  France, cardinal, 9, 12, 62, 65,
  87, 97, 100–1, 104–6

Eck, John, 60
Écouen, *château* of, 79; edict of
  (1559), 72
Edward VI, king of England, 43
Egypt, 9, 33
Eleanor (1498–1558) sister of the
  Emperor Charles V, successively
  queen of Portugal (1519–21)
  and of France (1530–47) as the
  2nd wife of Francis I, 26, 37,
  105, 114
Élections, 22
Elector palatine, 34, 102
Electors, imperial, 102–3
Elizabeth of Valois, queen of Spain,
  daughter of Henry II, 45, 72
Emmanuel-Philibert, duke of Savoy,
  45
Empire, *see* Holy Roman Empire
England, 1, 9, 34–5, 37–8, 43–5,
  56, 97; king of, 13
entries, royal, 75, 79, 82
Épargne, Trésor de l', 55
Erasmus, Desiderius (1466–1536),
  humanist, 60, 61–2
estates, imperial, 67
estates, provincial, 49, 88–9, 91,
  93–4, 96
Estates-General, 88–9
  (1483), 12
Este, Ippolito d', cardinal, 81, 115
Estienne, Robert, king's printer,
  85
Étampes, Anne d'Heilly (1508–80)
  duchess of, mistress of Francis I,
  27–8, 112, 114–15
evangelical humanism, 60–1
Évocations, 87
expedients, fiscal, 50, 55, 87, 96

Fantuzzi, Antonio, engraver, 80
Farel, Guillaume (1489–1565), 60, 64, 66
Febvre, Lucien (1878–1956), historian, 61
Ferdinand, king of Aragon, 31–2, 86
Ferdinand (1503–64), King of the Romans, brother of the Emperor Charles V, 38, 44
Ferrara, duchy of, 30; cardinal of, *see* Este, Ippolito d'
Fichet, Guillaume, 59
Field of Cloth of Gold (1520), 35, 47
fiscal administration, 20–3, 53, 55, 57
Flanders, 1, 2, 37
Fleming, Lady, 28
Florence, 30–2, 80, 87
Foix, Odet de (1481?–1528), *seigneur* de Lautrec, marshal of France, governor of Guyenne, 19, 35, 37, 48, 103–4
Fontainebleau, *château* of, 78–82, 85, 112; edict of (1540), 68
Forêt, Jean de la, 39
Forez, 11
Fornovo, battle of (1495), 31
fortresses, 56
Franche-Comté, 31–2, 34, 42
Francis I (1494–1547), king of France (1515–47), 24–6, 50, 52, 55, 61, 66–7, 78–9, 81–5, 88–9, 110, 113
Francis II (1544–60), king of France, son of Henry II, 24, 29, 43
Franciscans, 60
François (1518–36), eldest son of Francis I, 3, 27
Frankfurt, 103
Fribourg, 'perpetual peace' of (1516), 33, 48
Froben, John, printer of Basel, 60
Fugger, the, of Augsburg, 34, 102

Gabelle, 20–1, 49, 53, 57, 90
Gaillon, *château* of, 76
Garamond, Claude, 85
Gascony, 2, 98
gendarmerie, 20, 103
General Council of the Church, 38–9
Généralité(s), 22, 56
Geneva, 70–1, 98
Genoa (Genoese), 30–1, 33, 37, 45, 107
Germany, 38–9, 41–2, 67–8, 97, 103
Ghent, 41, 90, 111
Gouberville, Gilles de, 4
Gouffier, Guillaume (d. 1525), *seigneur* de Bonnivet, admiral of France, 35, 102–3
Goujon, Jean (1510?–1568), sculptor, 82
gouvernement(s), 19
grain, 5, 6, 9, 56, 107
Grand Almoner, 107
Grand conseil, 14, 62, 87, 106
Grand maître (Grand Master), 52, 73–4
Grand Parti de Lyon, 58
Grande Rebeine, 107
Grands Jours, 18, 92, 94, 102
Granvelle, Antoine Perrenot, cardinal de, 114
Graveron, dame de, 71
Grecs du roi, 85
Greek, study of, 83
Grenetier, 22
Grenier(s) à sel, 21–2, 57, 90
Grenoble, *parlement* of, 18
Grignan, Louis Adhémar, *seigneur* de, 114
Guillart, Charles, president of the *Parlement*, 102–3
Guise, Charles de, archbishop of Rheims, cardinal of Lorraine, 28, 43, 70, 79, 114–15
Guise, François de, count, later duke of Aumale, then duke of, 28, 43–5, 114–15

Guise, house of (Guises), 28–9, 43–4

Guise, Jean de, cardinal of Lorraine, 112, 115

Guyenne, 49, 57, 69

Habsburg, house of (Habsburgs), 30, 34, 38–9, 97

Haguenau, 43

Hamon, Philippe, historian, 50

Harlay, Louis de, *seigneur* de Beaumont, 106

Hauser, Henri, historian, 88

Hebrew, study of, 83

Henry II (1519–59), king of France (1547–59), previously duke of Orleans, 12, 15, 18, 26–8, 38–40, 42–4, 49, 58, 70–2, 75, 79, 81–3, 85, 90, 112, 114–15

Henry III (1551–89), king of France, 85

Henry IV, king of France(1589–1610), 58

Henry VIII, king of England (1509–47), 4, 31, 34–8, 42–3, 47, 55, 74

heresy (heretics), 13, 17, 38, 45, 60–1, 63–71, 87, 92, 110

Hesse, Philip, landgrave of, 39

Holy Roman Empire, 1, 11, 30, 34, 43–4, 102; *see also* Estates, imperial

Holy See, *see* Papacy

hospitals, 7–8

Huguenots, 71–2

Humanism, 59, 61

Hundred Years' War, 5, 8, 76

Ibrahim pasha, Ottoman grand vizier, 39

iconoclasm, 63, 106

Île-de-France, 6

Index of Forbidden Books, 69

industry, 7, 10

Infidel, *see* Turks

Inquisition, 70

Institutes of the Christian Religion, 68–9

Institution du prince, L', 14, 86

iron production, 11

Italians, 50, 55, 74, 80–1

Italy, 4, 8–10, 26, 29–39, 41–2, 44–5, 47, 64, 87, 107, 118–19

Jean I, duke of Bourbon, 3

Jeanne de France (1464-1505), first queen of Louis XII, 25

Juges-délégués, 63

Julius II (Giuliano della Rovere), pope (1503–13), 31

Karlstadt, Andreas, reformer, 64

King's household, *see Maison du roi*,

Kingship, 12–13, 94, 96

l'Aubespine, Claude de, 114

La Bicocca, battle of (1522), 35, 48

La Garde, Antoine Escalin des Essars, baron of (called 'Captain Polin'), 114

La Muette, *château* of, 78

La Rochelle, 9, 90, 110–11

Lagny-sur-Marne, 111

Landriano, battle of (1529), 37

Landsknechts, 48

Languedoc, 2, 9, 18, 22, 41, 49, 90, 92–3; estates of, 50, 94–5; governor of, 20

Languedoïl, 1, 2, 22

Lannoy, Charles de (1482–1527), viceroy of Naples, 35–6, 104

Laon cathedral, 52

Lautrec, Marshal, *see* Foix, Odet de

law, 2, 13, 69, 95, 99

laws, fundamental, 16, 51

Le Havre, 9

Lecteurs royaux, 83

Lefèvre d'Étaples, Jacques (1450–1536), scholar, 26, 59–65

Legions, provincial, 39, 49

Leipzig, 60

Leo X (Giovanni de' Medici), pope (1513–21), 32–3, 35, 47, 50, 60, 86–7, 102

Leonardo da Vinci (1452–1519), artist, 76, 80

Lescot, Pierre (1510?–1575), architect, 77–9

Lettre(s) de jussion, 17, 18, 91

Leucate, 41

Limoges, 4

Limours, 114

Lisieux, bishop of, 107

Lit de justice, 16, 72, 75, 88–9, 91

Loans, 50–3, 55, 58, 102

Lombard, Peter (1100?–1164), 60

Lombardy, 37, 42

London, treaty of (1518), 35

Longueval, Nicolas de Bossut, *seigneur* de, 114

Lorges, Jacques de Montgommery, *seigneur* de, 111

Lorraine, 43, 102

Lorraine, cardinal of, *see* Guise, Charles de, and Jean de

Lorraine, duke of, 1

Louis XI, king of France (1461–83), 10

Louis XII, king of France (1498–1515), previously duke of Orleans, 2, 31, 49, 69, 84

Louis XIV, king of France (1643–1715) 15, 86, 95–6

Louis XV, king of France (1715–74), 78

Louise of Savoy (1476–1531), mother of Francis I, twice regent of France, 3–4, 12, 24–6, 31, 36–7, 53, 62, 87, 89, 103–5

Louise, daughter of Francis I, 32

Louvre, The, 56, 64, 72, 77, 79, 81–2, 108

Low Countries, 9, 31–2, 34, 41–2, 44–5, 59, 80

Luther, Martin (1483–1546), reformer, 60–2, 64

Lutheran, use of the name, 67

Lutheranism (Lutherans), 60–2, 65, 117

Luxemburg, 27, 35, 42

Lyonnais, 17, 49

Lyons, 4, 6–8, 10–11, 50, 55–6, 58, 62, 69, 79, 82, 107

Madrid, *château* of, 77

Madrid, peace of (1526), 2, 4, 26–7, 36–7, 43, 88–9, 104–5

Mainz, archbishop of, 34

Maison du roi, 73

Maîtres des requêtes de l'hôtel, 15

Major, J. Russell, historian, 86, 88

Mantua, duke of, 79

Marchaumont, 114

Marcillac, François de, president of the *parlement* of Rouen, 91

Marcourt, Antoine, 66

Margaret of Savoy (1480–1530), regent in the Netherlands, aunt of the Emperor Charles V, 37

Marguerite d'Angoulême (1492–1549), duchess of Alençon, then (1527) queen of Navarre, sister of Francis I, 26, 61, 63–4, 112

Marguerite (1523–74), daughter of Francis I, later duchess of Savoy, 26, 45

Maria, daughter of the Emperor Charles V, 42

Marignano, battle of (1515), 32, 47–8, 86

Marot, Clément (1496–1544) poet, 65, 84

Marseilles, 8, 36, 38, 40

Mary Stuart (1542–87), queen of France, wife of Francis II, 43

Mary Tudor (1516–58), queen of England, 44–5, 118

Mary Tudor (1496–1533), sister of Henry VIII, 2nd queen of Louis XII, then duchess of Suffolk, 25

Maubert, place, Paris, 116

Maximilian I, Holy Roman Emperor (1493–1519), 31, 33–4, 47, 102
Mazurier, Martial, 60, 62
Meaux, 69
Medici, Cosimo de', duke of Florence (1537–74), 45
Medici, house of, 30–2, 87
Mehmet II, Ottoman sultan (1551–81), 33
Melanchthon, Philip (1497–1560), reformer, 62
Menu peuple, 7–8
mercenaries, 31, 33, 47–9
merchants, 7, 10, 21, 50, 74, 107
Mérindol, 69–70
metallurgy, 10
Metz, 2, 43–5
Meudon, grotto of, 79
Mézières, 35
Michelangelo (1475–1564) sculptor and painter, 80–1
Michelet, Jules, historian (1798–1874), 24, 28
Milan, 11, 32–3, 35–7, 41, 80, 107; duchy of, 30–1, 34, 40, 42, 47, 86, 103
Milan, Pierre, engraver, 80
mining, 10
Mirror of a Sinful Soul, 26, 64
Monarchie de France, La, 14
Monarchy, *see* Kingship
Monluc, Blaise de (1499?–1577), marshal of France, 98
Montmorency, Anne de (1493–1567), successively Grand Master and Constable of France, 20, 27–8, 40–1, 43–5, 48, 70, 74, 79, 104, 106, 114–15, 119
Montpellier, 33; ordinance of (1537), 84
Montreuil, 42
Montrevel, Jean de La Baume, count of, 114
Monzón, truce of (1537), 41

More, treaty of the (1525), 36
Mothe-au-Groing, *seigneur* de la, 108
Muley Hassan, ruler of Tunis, 39
Mysticism, 59

Nantes, 6, 9
Naples, 37, 44; kingdom of, 29–34, 47, 86; viceroy of *see* Lannoy, Charles de *and* Alba, Fernando Alvarez de Toledo, 3rd duke of
Napoleon, 78
Nassau, Henry, count of (1483–1538), 35, 40, 103
Navarre, *collège* de, 64
Navarre, king of, *see* Albret, Jean d' *and* Bourbon, Antoine de; kingdom of, 1, 32–3, 35
navy, 56
Netherlands, *see* Low Countries
Neuchâtel, 64, 66
Nice, 41–2; truce of (1538), 41, 68
Nivernais, 49
nobility (nobles), 7, 19–20, 48, 71–3, 76, 78, 93–4, 96, 106
nobility, titles of, 50–1
Nominalism, 59
Normandy, 4, 9, 17, 22, 49, 69, 92; estates of, 93; governor of, 114; *Grand sénéchal* of, 104, 106
Notables, Assembly of (1527), 89
Notre-Dame, Paris, 69, 106
Novara, battle of (1513), 31
Noyon, treaty of (1516), 32–3

office-holders, 7, 12, 15, 51
offices, royal, 13, 15, 17–18, 50–1, 54, 91, 95–6, 102, 106
Olivier, François, chancellor of France, 114
Oppède, Jean Maynier, baron d', 70
Orange, principality of, 1
Orders, 80
Orleans, house of, 31
Orval, Jean d'Albret, *seigneur* d', 102–03

Pagès, Georges, historian, 86
Papacy, 1, 10, 34, 100, 118
Paris, 6, 7, 9, 11, 17, 20, 50, 59,
   62–3, 66, 72, 74, 77, 84–5, 94,
   100–2, 106
Paris, university of, 59, 64–5, 87;
   see also Sorbonne
Parisians, 69, 75
Paris, *Parlement* of, 3, 14, 16–19,
   51, 54, 62–5, 67, 69–70, 72, 75,
   87–9, 91, 97, 100, 102, 105–8,
   111–12
Parlements, 2, 7, 16, 18–19, 68–9,
   88–9, 91, 94–6, 98–9, 102, *see*
   also under the names of towns
   with a parlement
Parmigianino, Francesco, il
   (1503–40), 79
Passau, diet of, 44
Paul III (Alessandro Farnese), pope
   (1534–49), 39–41
Paul IV (Giampietro Carafa), pope
   (1555–59), 44, 118
Pavia, 36; battle of (1525), 26, 36,
   48, 52, 62, 87
Pays d' états, 22, 92, 94
Pays de grandes gabelles, 21–2, 57,
peasantry, 5–6, 21, 69, 96
Pellicier, Guillaume, French
   ambassador in Venice, 84
Péronne, 40
Perpignan, 27, 42
Petit Nesle, 112
Petit, Guillaume, 83
Philip, son of the Emperor Charles
   V, later Philip II of Spain, 41,
   44–5, 72, 118
Picardy, 9, 49
Piedmont, 29, 40–2, 45, 56, 60
Pitti collection, Florence, 81
Placards, Affair of the (1534), 39,
   65–7, 108–9
Pléiade, the, 85
poetry, 84–85
Poitiers, 87; Calvinist synod of,
   71

Poitou, 9, 90
Poland, king of, 102
Polin, Captain, *see* La Garde
political thought, 14
Pollard, A.F., historian, 35
Poncher, Jean, treasurer of
   Languedoc, 54
poor, 7–8, 108
Pope, 30, 32, 34
ports, 9
Pot, Philippe, 12
Poyet, Guillaume (1473–1548),
   chancellor of France, 91, 95
Pragmatic Sanction of Bourges
   (1438), 32, 87, 100
Pré-aux-Clercs, 72
Prentout, Henri, historian, 86
Présidiaux, 18–19, 92
Prévôts, 16
prices, 6, 8, 107
Primaticcio, Francesco
   (1504/5–1570), 79, 81
printing, 11, 85
Protestantism, 26, 67, 70–71
Provence, 1, 2, 4, 8, 20, 36, 40–1,
   49, 60, 69, 90, 92, 114
provincial governors, 19–20, 96

Rabelais, François (1483?–1553),
   author, 84
Radical Reformation, 63
Rambouillet, 114
Raphael (1483–1520), artist, 80
Realism, 59
Recettes-générales, 56
remonstrances, 17–18, 63, 87
Renée de France (1510–75),
   duchess of Ferrara, daughter of
   King Louis XII, 102
Rennes, *parlement* of, 18
Rentes sur l'Hôtel de Ville de Paris,
   52–3
Renty, battle of (1554), 118
Résignations, 51
revenue, 57
Rheims, 13; archbishop of, 13

Rhétoriqueurs, 84

Robertet, Florimond (d.1527), royal secretary, 106

Romano, Giulio (1492–1546), painter, 79

Rome, 38, 40, 45, 80–2, 84, 107; sack of, 4, 36–7

Ronsard, Pierre de (1524–85), poet, 85

Rosso, Giovanni Battista (1494–1540), artist, 78, 80

Rouen, 6, 7, 9, 90–1; archbishop of, 92; Henry II's entry into, 82–3; *parlement* of, 18, 91–2, 95, 102

Roussel, Gérard (1480–1550), 60, 63–4

Roussillon, 1

Rubens, Peter Paul (1577–1640), painter, 82

Sacramentarianism, Sacramentarians, 63, 66–8, 110

Saint-Denis, abbey of, 79, 82

Saint-Dizier, 42

Saint-Germain-en-Laye, *château* of, 76

Saint-Jacques, rue, affair of the (1557), 71, 116

Saint-Maur-les-Fossés, *château* of, 79

Saint-Mauris, Jean de, imperial ambassador, 114

Saint-Pol, François de Bourbon (1491–1545), *comte* de, 37, 106

Saint-Quentin, 45, 117; battle of (1557), 45, 58

Saintonge, 90

Salic Law, 25

Salt tax, *see Gabelle*

salt, 9, 21, 90

Saluzzo, Francesco, marquis of, 40

Sarto, Andrea del (1486–1531), painter, 80

Savoy, duchy of, 2, 30, 40, 45

Savoy, René of (d. 1525), Grand Master of France, 87

Saxony, duke of, 34, 102; Maurice, duke of, 44

Scandinavia, 9

Schmalkaldic League (1531), 38

Scholasticism (Schoolmen), 59–60

Scotland (Scots), 42–3, 118

Scottish guard, 74

sculpture, 81, 82

Seaford, 43

Secrétaire(s) des finances, 15

Secretaries of state, 15, 74, 78, 114

Selim the Grim, Ottoman sultan (1512–20), 33

Semblançay, *see* Beaune, Jacques de

Sénéchal, Sénéchaux, 11, 16, 89

Sénéchaussée, 7, 16, 102

Sens, archbishop of, *see* Duprat, Antoine; *bailli* of, 116 receiver of, 114;

Seyssel, Claude de (1450–1520), bishop of Marseilles, 4, 14, 98

Sforza, Francesco (1495–1535), duke of Milan, 40

Sforza, house of, 30–1

Sforza, Massimiliano (1491–1530), duke of Milan, 31–2, 47

Sicily, 30, 39

Siena, 45, 93

silk, 7, 9–10

Somerset, Edward Seymour, Protector, 43

Sorbonne, 59–65, 67–9, 84, 116

Sovereign courts, 14, 70, 99

Spain, 8–9, 27, 33–4, 36, 41, 43, 45, 54, 63, 83, 89; king of, 102

spices, 10

St Benoît-sur-Loire, abbot of, *see* Duprat, Antoine

St Michael, Order of, 114

St Louis, 3

Standonck, John, 59

States of the Church (Papal states), 30, 44, 87

Strassburg (Strasbourg), 43, 71

Strozzi, Piero (d. 1556), 114
Suleiman 'the Magnificent', Ottoman
    sultan (1520–66), 39, 41
Survivances, 51
Susa, Val di, 41
Swiss, 31–3, 47–8, 50, 55, 68, 74,
    103
Switzerland, 48, 64–6, 68
Synod, national (1559), 72

Taille, 20, 49, 52, 56, 93
Taillon, 93
taxation, 7, 8, 13, 20, 49–50, 55,
    90–1, 94, 96–7, 103; resistance
    to, 57, 90
Tenth, clerical, *see Décime*
textiles, 9
Thenaud, Jean, 83
Touch, royal, 13
Toul, 2, 43
Toulon, 42, 45
Toulouse, 6–7, 9, 50; *parlement* of,
    2, 18, 69, 102
Tour Carrée, commission de la, 54
Tournai, 47
Tournaisis, 2
Tournon, François de (1489–1562),
    cardinal, 28, 55–6, 70, 113–15
Tours, 7, 52
towns, 4–5, 7, 10, 13, 20–1, 49,
    51–2, 55–6, 69, 88, 94, 96,
    100–1
trade, 7–9, 11, 94
Trésor, 22
Trésorier de l'Épargne, 53, 57
Trésoriers de France, 22, 51, 54
Tribolo, Niccolò, sculptor, 81
Trier, archbishop of, 34, 102
Trivulzio, Gian-Giacomo (1448–
    1518), marshal of France, 32
Troyes, 50
Tuileries, palace of the, 72, 79

Tunis, 39
Turks, 33, 38–9, 41–2, 67
Turquet, Étienne, 10

vagabondage, 6, 11
Valois, house of, 24
Vasari, Giorgio (1511–74), painter
    and writer, 80
Vatican palace, Rome, 76, 81
Vaucelles, truce of (1556), 44
Vaudois, *see* Waldensians
Vendôme, 73
Venetians, 31
Venice, 8, 30–1, 80, 87
Verdun, 2, 43–5
Vienna, 80–1
Vignola, Giacomo Barozzi da
    (1507–73), architect, 81
Villers-Cotterêts, *château* of, 79;
    ordinance of (1539), 11, 91
villes-franches, 20
Vincennes, forest of, 100
Visconti, house of, 31
Vitruvius, (1st c.AD) roman
    architect, 79

wages, 6, 8, 11, 17
Waldensians (Waldensianism), 60,
    69
war, cost of, 47, 52, 54, 56
Wars of Religion, 5, 46, 96
Warwick, John Dudley, earl of,
    43
Wight, Isle of, 43
wine, 9, 21, 51
Wolsey, Thomas (1475?–1530),
    cardinal, 26, 34–6, 38, 55
Württemberg, 38–9; Ulrich, duke
    of, 39, 55

Zwingli, Huldrych (1484–1531),
    Swiss reformer, 63–4